MUMMY
MUSIC
MYTHOLOGY
NASCAR
NATURAL DISASTERS
NORTH AMERICAN INDIAN
OCEAN
OIL
OLYMPICS
PERSPECTIVE
PHOTOGRAPHY
PIRATE
...DENTS
PYRAMID
RELIGION
RENAISSANCE
REPTILE
RESCUE
ROBOT
ROCKS & MINERALS
RUSSIA
SEASHORE
SHAKESPEARE
SHARK
SHELL
SHIPWRECK
SKELETON
SOCCER
SPACE EXPLORATION
SPORTS
SPY
SUBMARINE
SUPER BOWL
TECHNOLOGY
TEXAS
TIME & SPACE
TITANIC
TRAIN
TREE
UNIVERSE
VAN GOGH
VIETNAM WAR
VIKING
VOLCANOES & EARTHQUAKES
VOTE
WATERCOLOR
WEATHER
WHALE
WILD WEST
WITCHES & MAGIC-MAKERS
WORLD SERIES
WORLD WAR I
WORLD WAR II

Eyewitness
WEATHER

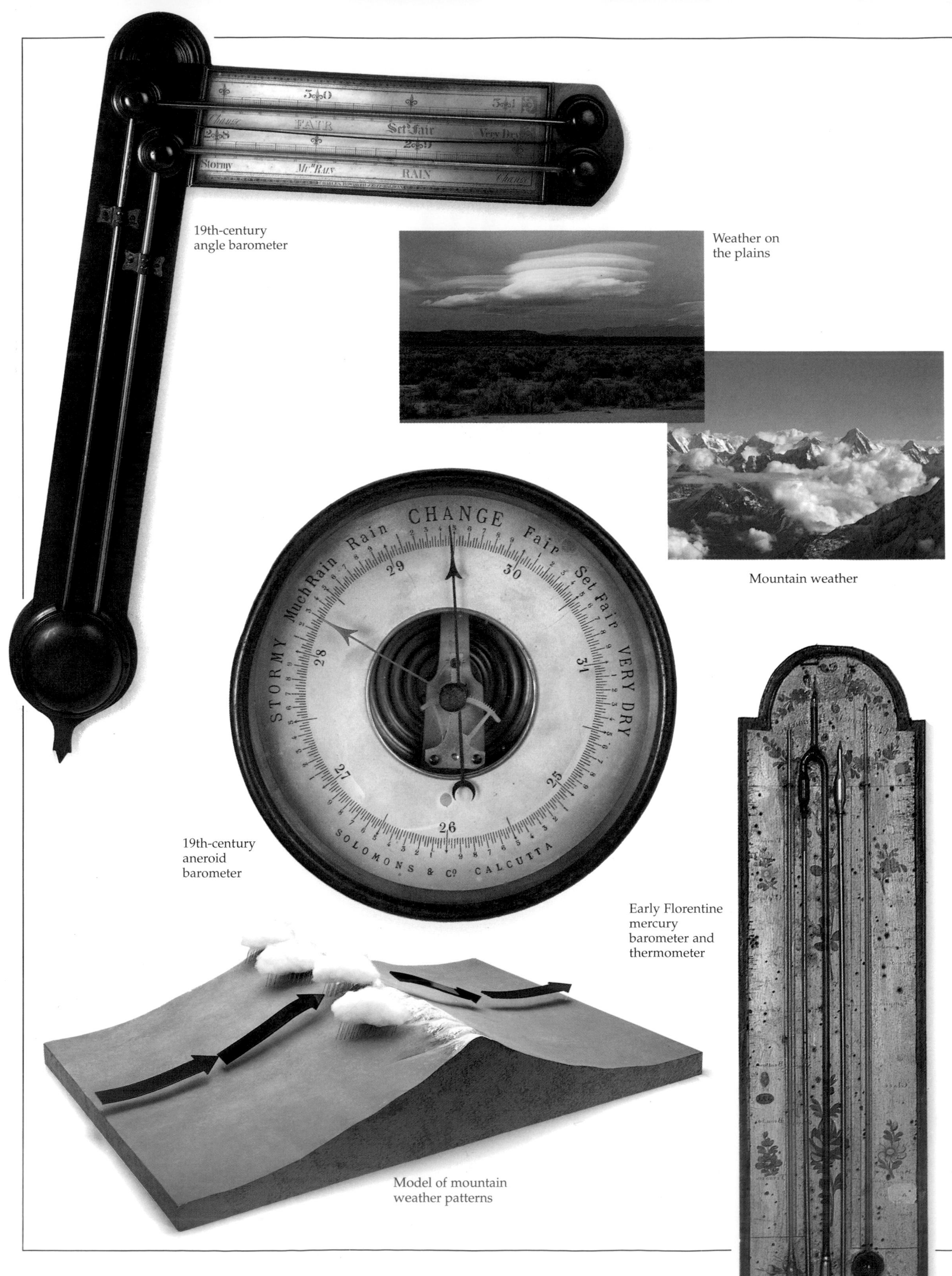

19th-century angle barometer

Weather on the plains

Mountain weather

19th-century aneroid barometer

Early Florentine mercury barometer and thermometer

Model of mountain weather patterns

Macrophotograph of a snow crystal

Eyewitness WEATHER

Written by
BRIAN COSGROVE

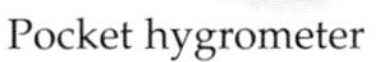

Pocket hygrometer

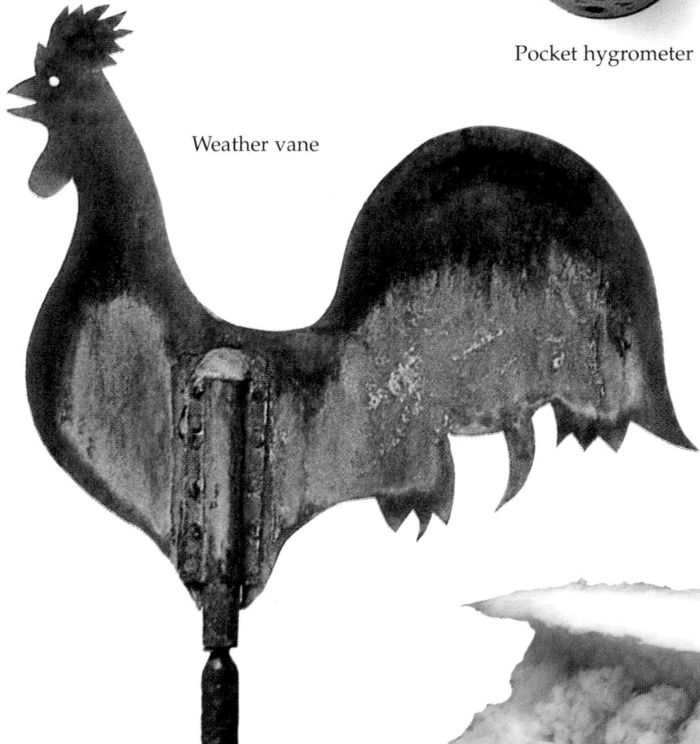

Weather vane

Early English thermometer

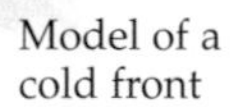

Model of a cold front

DK Publishing, Inc.

Statue of an Aztec sun god

Open and shut pinecones, indicating damp or dry weather

Quadrant

LONDON, NEW YORK,
MELBOURNE, MUNICH, and DELHI

Project editors John Farndon, Marion Dent
Art editor Alison Anholt-White
Senior editor Helen Parker
Senior art editors Jacquie Gulliver, Julia Harris
Production Louise Barratt
Picture research Diana Morris
Special photography Karl Shone, Keith Percival
Editorial consultant Jim Sharp

REVISED EDITION
Managing editors Andrew Macintyre, Camilla Hallinan
Managing art editors Jane Thomas, Martin Wilson
Publishing manager Sunita Gahir
Category publisher Andrea Pinnington
Editors Angela Wilkes, Sue Nicholson
Art editor Catherine Goldsmith
Production Jenny Jacoby, Georgina Hayworth
Picture research Sarah Pownall
DTP designers Siu Chan, Andy Hilliard, Ronaldo Julien

U.S. editor Elizabeth Hester
Senior editor Beth Sutinis
Art director Dirk Kaufman
U.S. production Chris Avgherinos
U.S. DTP designer Milos Orlovic

This Eyewitness ® Guide has been conceived by
Dorling Kindersley Limited and Editions Gallimard

This edition published in the United States in 2007
by DK Publishing, Inc., 375 Hudson Street, New York, New York 10014

08 10 9 8 7 6 5 4
WD149 - 04/07

Published in Great Britain by Dorling Kindersley Limited.

A catalog record for this book is available from the Library of Congress.

ISBN 978-0-7566-3006-5 (HC) 978-0-7566-0737-1 (Library Binding)

Color reproduction by Colourscan, Singapore
Printed in China by Toppan Printing Co. (Shenzhen), Ltd.

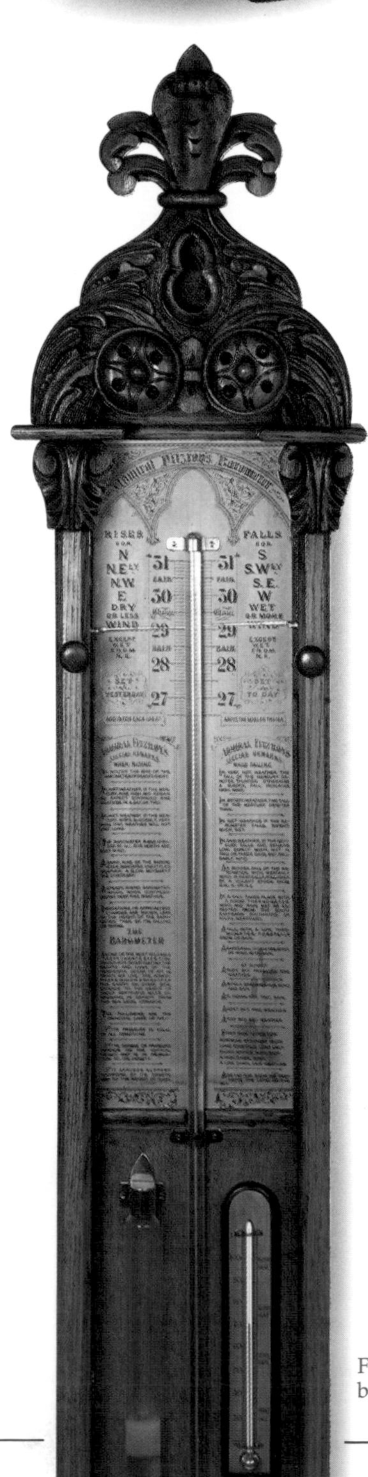
Fitzroy barometer

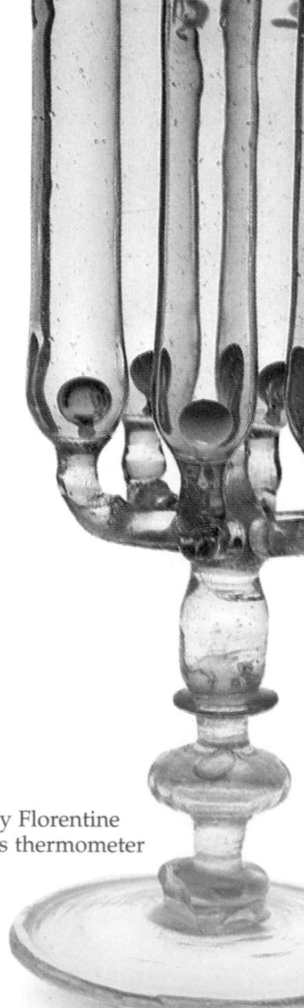
Early Florentine glass thermometer

Discover more at

www.dk.com

Contents

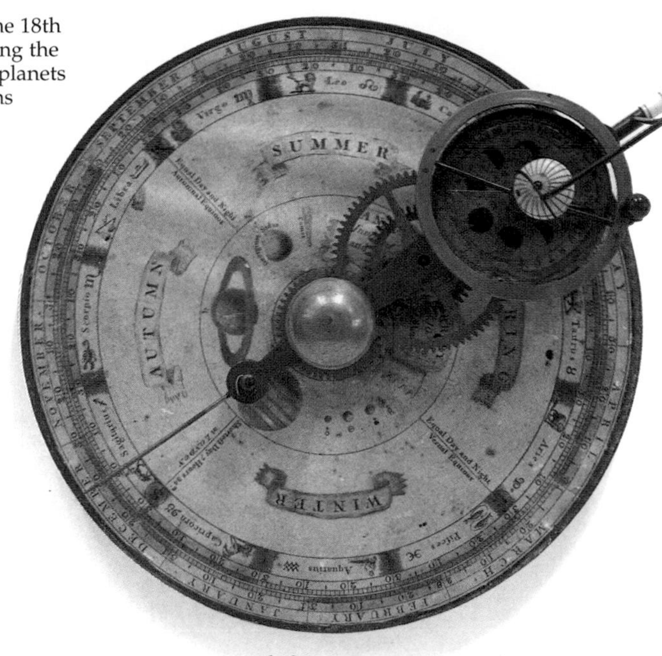
Orrery from the 18th century showing the motion of the planets and the seasons

The restless air

OUR PLANET IS SURROUNDED by a blanket of gases called the atmosphere. If it were not for the atmosphere we would not be able to live – we would be burned by the intense heat of the daytime sun or frozen by the icy chill of night. Look into the sky on a clear day, and you can see the atmosphere stretching some 600 miles (1,000 km) above you. Perhaps 99 percent of it is as calm and unchanging as space beyond. But the very lowest layer, 6 miles (10 km) high – the air in which we live and breathe – is forever on the move, boiling and bubbling in the sun's heat like a vast kettle on a fire. It is the constant swirling and stirring of this lowest layer of the atmosphere, called the troposphere, which gives us everything we call weather, from the warm, still days of summer to the wildest storms of winter.

TAKING THE AIR
James Glaisher and Robert Coxwell were just two of many brave researchers who, in the 19th century, risked their lives in balloons to find out about the atmosphere. They found that the air got colder the higher they went. By 1902, though, unmanned balloons had proved it gets colder with height only up to a point called the tropopause – the top of the troposphere.

BREATH OF LIFE
The nature of air intrigued scientists for centuries. Then, in the 1770s, Joseph Priestley's experiments with mice showed that air contains something that animals need to live. Like many, he thought this was a substance called phlogiston.

PLANET OF CLOUDS
In photographs from space, great swirls of clouds can be seen enveloping the Earth. These swirls dramatically highlight the constant motion of gases in the troposphere that gives us our weather. Many of the world's major weather patterns can be seen clearly. Along the equator, for instance, is a ribbon of clouds thousands of miles long, formed because the intense heat of the sun here stirs up strong updrafts. These carry moisture from the ocean so high into the air that it cools and condenses to form clouds (pp. 24-25).

WHAT IS AIR?
In the 1780s, French chemist Antoine Lavoisier found that Priestley's vital "something" was a gas, which he called oxygen. He also found that air contained two other gases – nitrogen and carbon dioxide. Later, air was found to be roughly 21% oxygen, 78% nitrogen, and less than 1% carbon dioxide and other gases.

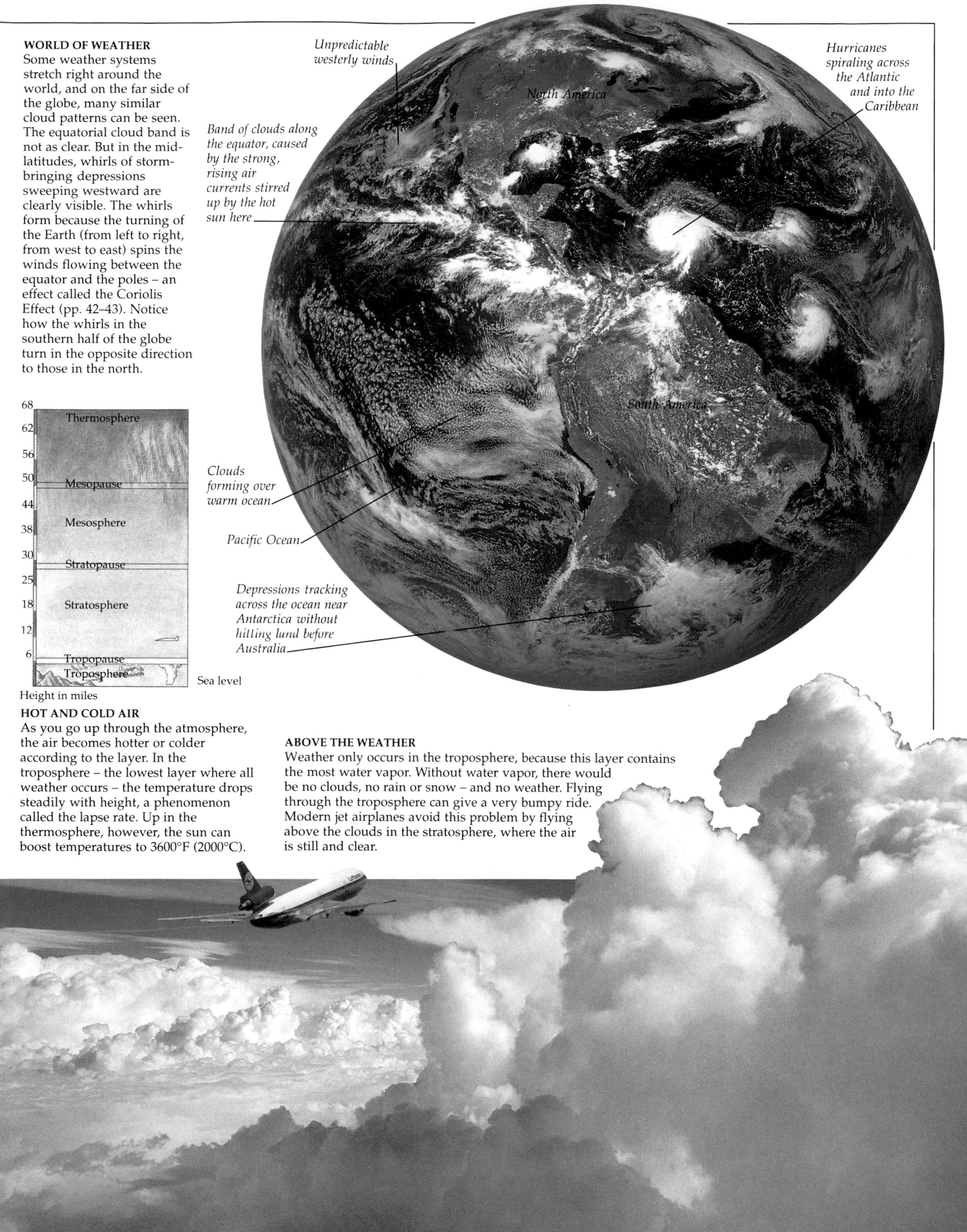

WORLD OF WEATHER
Some weather systems stretch right around the world, and on the far side of the globe, many similar cloud patterns can be seen. The equatorial cloud band is not as clear. But in the mid-latitudes, whirls of storm-bringing depressions sweeping westward are clearly visible. The whirls form because the turning of the Earth (from left to right, from west to east) spins the winds flowing between the equator and the poles – an effect called the Coriolis Effect (pp. 42–43). Notice how the whirls in the southern half of the globe turn in the opposite direction to those in the north.

HOT AND COLD AIR
As you go up through the atmosphere, the air becomes hotter or colder according to the layer. In the troposphere – the lowest layer where all weather occurs – the temperature drops steadily with height, a phenomenon called the lapse rate. Up in the thermosphere, however, the sun can boost temperatures to 3600°F (2000°C).

ABOVE THE WEATHER
Weather only occurs in the troposphere, because this layer contains the most water vapor. Without water vapor, there would be no clouds, no rain or snow – and no weather. Flying through the troposphere can give a very bumpy ride. Modern jet airplanes avoid this problem by flying above the clouds in the stratosphere, where the air is still and clear.

Natural signs

FOR CENTURIES, SAILORS, FARMERS, and others whose livelihood depends on the weather have known that the world around them gives all kinds of clues to the weather to come – as long as they know what to look for. Age-old advice passed down from generation to generation has been offered on everything from the color of the sky to the feel of your boots in the morning. Of course, some country weather lore is little more than superstition and all but useless for weather forecasting. But much is based on close observation of the natural world and can give an accurate prediction of the weather. Tiny variations in the air, which we cannot feel, often affect plants and animals. A change in their appearance or behavior can be the sign of a change in the weather.

WHAT'S THE WEATHER LIKE?
Everyone – from travelers to sailors – had to know about the weather and be aware of natural signs around them.

NOTHING BUT A GROUNDHOG *above*
In the USA, February 2 is Groundhog Day. People say that if a groundhog sees its shadow, the weather will remain cold for six more weeks. Happily, weather records have proved the groundhog wrong many times.

SUN DAY OPENING
The scarlet pimpernel is often known as the "poor man's weather glass." Its tiny flowers open wide in sunny weather, but close up tightly when rain is in the air.

Sunset

Sunrise

SEEING RED
Old seafarers' wisdom says, *Red sky at night, sailors' delight; red sky at morning, sailors take warning* – which means a fiery sunset should be followed by a clear morning, and a fiery dawn by storms. This is one folk saying that is often true.

WEATHER WEED
People near the sea often hang out strands of kelp, for seaweed is one of the best natural weather forecasters. In fine weather, the kelp shrivels and is dry to the touch. If rain (pp. 30–31) threatens, the weed swells and feels damp.

CURLY WARNING
Wool is very responsive to the humidity, or moistness, of the air. When the air is dry, wool shrinks and curls up. If rain is on its way, the air is moist, and wool swells and straightens out.

CRICKET FORECAST
Like many small creatures, grasshoppers are sensitive to changes in the weather, chirruping louder and louder as the temperature rises. The chirruping is not actually a song, but the sound of the grasshoppers' hind legs rubbing rapidly against their hard front wings.

GLORIOUS MORNING
Like the scarlet pimpernel, the petals of morning glory open and shut in response to weather conditions. These wide-open blooms indicate fine weather.

WEATHER CONES
A pine cone is one of the most reliable of all natural weather indicators. In dry weather, the scales on a pine cone open out; when they close up, it is a good sign that rain is on the way. This is because, in dry weather, the scales shrivel up and stand out stiffly. When the air is damp, the scales absorb moisture and become pliable again, allowing the cone to regain its normal shape.

SOAK OR SPLASH?
According to some country weather lore, natural signs can indicate the weather, not just for the next few hours but for many days to come. An old English saying, for instance, is: *If the oak flowers before the ash, we shall have a splash* (meaning only light rain for the next month or so). *If the ash flowers before the oak, we shall have a soak* (meaning very wet weather). There is little evidence, however, to support any of these long-range predictions.

LYING COWS
When you see cows lying down in a field, it is sometimes said that rain must be on the way. Apparently, the cows sense the dampness in the air and are making sure they have somewhere dry to lie. While many animals can indeed sense changes in the weather before humans, this particular prediction proves wrong as often as right.

SPRING IS HERE
Many natural signs are said to herald the end of winter. One of the best known is the first blooming of the white flowers of the horse chestnut. It is true that the flowers will only appear once the weather is mild enough – but this is no guarantee that there will be no more winter storms.

WINTER'S TAIL
Some country folk expect a severe winter if in autumn squirrels have very bushy tails, or gather big stores of nuts. But scientists have found no evidence to support this.

The science of weather

WEATHER AND THE ATMOSPHERE attracted the attention of thinkers and academics as long ago as the days of ancient Greece. It was the Greek philosopher Aristotle who gave us the word "meteorology" for the scientific study of weather. In the 17th century, in Renaissance Italy, the first instruments were developed to measure changes in the temperature of the air, its pressure, or weight, and its moisture content. It was in Italy, around 1600, that the great astronomer and mathematician Galileo Galilei made the first thermometer. Called the thermoscope, it was notoriously inaccurate. Some 40 years later, Galileo's secretary-assistant Torricelli made the first practical barometer for measuring the pressure of the air. The first really successful thermometer was one made by German physicist Daniel Fahrenheit in about 1709 using alcohol, followed in 1714 by one he made using mercury. He also produced some of the earliest meteorological instruments for studying the weather.

HEAT BALLS
Perhaps the first to prove that air expands when heated was Philo, a philosopher from the 2nd century B.C., who lived in Byzantium (now Istanbul in Turkey). When he connected a pipe from a hollow lead ball to a jug of water, air bubbled through the water when the ball was heated by the sun.

Water-absorbent paper disks

Pivot

Scale indicating humidity

WET OR DRY
In the 17th and 18th centuries people tried all kinds of ingenious ways of measuring the air's invisible moisture content. This simple hygrometer does just that. It is an English instrument dating from the early 18th century and consists of a balance with a pile of soft paper disks on one arm. If the air is dry, the disks dry out and weigh less. If the air is humid, they absorb water and weigh more, pulling the pointer up.

ICY WATER
This replica of one of the earliest accurate hygrometers, designed by Grand Duke Ferdinand II in 1657, has a hollow core that can be filled with ice. Moisture in the air condenses on the outside and runs down into a measuring cylinder. The amount of water that is collected indicates the humidity of the air.

Flask for collecting water

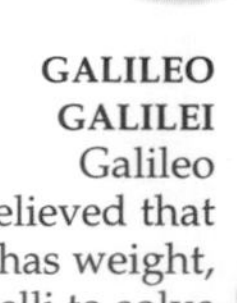

GALILEO GALILEI
Galileo believed that air has weight, and asked his assistant Torricelli to solve why a suction pump will not raise a column of water higher than about 9 m (30 ft). In solving this, Torrelli rejected conventional views and invented the barometer.

WEATHER ACADEMY

The *Accademia del Cimento* in Florence became the focus of early scientific study of the atmosphere. This painting shows members of the academy in 1657, conducting an experiment on heat and cold. Using a thermometer, a mirror, and a bucket of ice, they are trying to find out if cold, like heat, can be reflected. It cannot.

EARLY WEATHER

The Italian script of this early 18th-century barometer shows how clearly people understood the barometer's value for forecasting weather.

CROWN GLASS

Early Florentine meteorologists were served by the most skilled glass blowers in Europe, whose skill made many of the earliest instruments possible. This elaborate and beautiful thermometer dates from shortly after the time of Galileo. Temperatures are registered by the rise and fall of colored glass balls in the water within the tubes.

QUICKSILVER TUBE

This is a mercury barometer and thermometer, which became available in the early 18th century. Such barometers came into widespread use for measuring air pressure and worked by showing changes in the level of liquid quicksilver, or mercury, in a glass tube open to the air at the base. The level varies because when the air pressure is high, it weighs heavily on the mercury at the base, pushing it farther up the tube. When air pressure is low, the level of mercury drops.

EVANGELISTA TORRICELLI

In 1644, Torricelli made the first barometer and proved the existence of air pressure. He filled a 3-ft (1-m) glass tube with mercury, then held the open end under the surface in a bowl of mercury. The mercury in the tube dropped to about 32 in (80 cm), leaving a vacuum at the top of the tube. Torricelli realized it was the weight, or pressure, of air on the mercury in the bowl that stopped it from falling farther.

DIAL HYGROMETER

The needle of this early hygrometer is made to move by a paper strip which shrinks or stretches in response to the dampness of the air.

Watching the weather

MODERN WEATHER FORECASTING depends on gathering together and assessing millions of observations and measurements of atmospheric conditions, constantly recorded at the same time all over the world. No single system of measurements can give meteorologists a complete picture, so information is fed in from a wide range of sources. Most important are the many land-based weather stations, from city centers to remote islands. Ships and radio signals from drifting weather buoys report details of conditions at sea. Balloons and specially equipped airplanes take measurements up through the atmosphere, while out in space weather satellites constantly circle the Earth, beaming back pictures of cloud and temperature patterns.

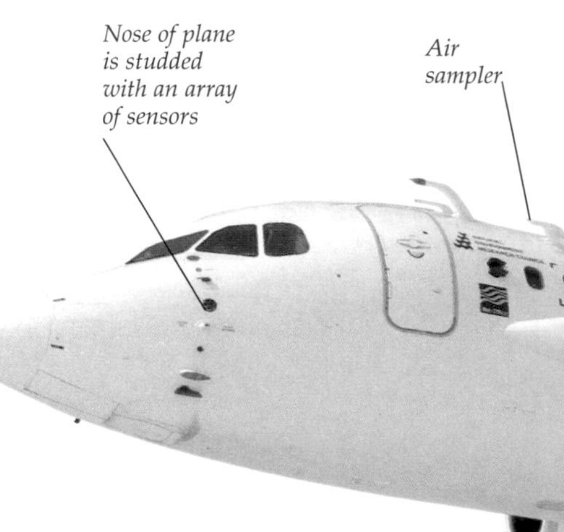

Atmospheric research aircraft

STORM TOSSED
The need for ships to have advance warning of storms at sea encouraged people to set up organized weather forecasting networks.

FIXED STATION
At the heart of the world's weather watching is a network of about 11,000 permanent weather stations, linked together by the World Meteorological Organization. Most of these stations send reports every three hours (called "synoptic hours") to a number of main weather centers around the world. The centers then pass on this weather data so that different countries can make up their own weather forecasts.

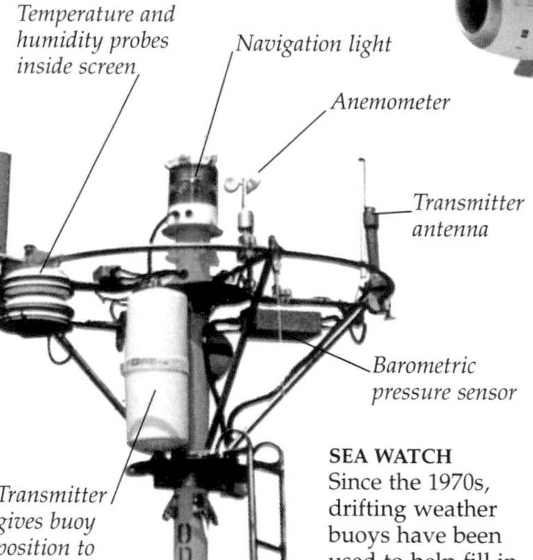

SEA WATCH
Since the 1970s, drifting weather buoys have been used to help fill in the gaps left by ship's observations about conditions at sea. There are about such 1,250 buoys, which float freely with the ocean currents and send readings back to land via satellites. The satellites can pinpoint where the buoy is to within 1 mile (2 km).

HIGH VIEW

Since 1960, satellite pictures have played a vital role in monitoring the weather. They provide two basic types of picture. Normal photographs show the Earth and clouds just as we would see them, while infrared pictures record infrared radiation to show temperatures at the nearest visible point.

"Blister" on fuselage houses radiation monitoring equipement

Sensors mounted on under-wing pylon

OUT OF THIS WORLD

There are two types of weather satellite. Geostationary satellites always remain fixed in the same spot, usually high above the equator, about 22,000 miles (36,000 km) out in space. There are eight of them altogether, providing an almost complete picture of the globe (except for the two poles) every half hour. Polar-orbiting satellites circle the Earth in strips from pole to pole. They have a lower orbit and provide a changing, more detailed weather picture from closer to the Earth's surface. In 2006, there were about 20 polar-orbiting satellites.

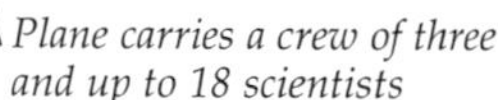

Plane carries a crew of three and up to 18 scientists

FLYING LABORATORY

Specially modified research aircraft are equipped with an array of sophisticated equipment to assess weather conditions at various levels in the atmosphere. In the US, there are even aircraft that are adapted so that they can fly right into the eye of a hurricane. This plane, operated by the UK's Facility for Airborne Atmospheric Measurements, is designed to take a wide range of readings concerning weather and climate, including levels of solar, microwave, and other radiation, and the atmospheric concentrations of ozone and "greenhouse" gases (pp. 60–61) such as carbon

Onboard scientist checking data

JOSEPH HENRY

In 1848, Joseph Henry of the Smithsonian Institution Washington, D.C., set up a system to obtain simultaneous weather reports from across the continent. By 1849, over 200 observers were taking measurements nationwide and sending them back to Mr. Henry in Washington. These were displayed on a large map in the Institution, and provided daily weather reports for the Washington Evening Post.

SKY PROBE

At midnight and noon Greenwich Mean Time, hundreds of helium, gas-filled balloons are launched into the upper atmosphere all around the world. As they rise higher and higher, automatic instruments frequently take humidity, pressure, and temperature readings. These are radioed to the ground and the instrument package is called a radiosonde. Wind speed at various heights can be calculated by tracking the way the balloon rises.

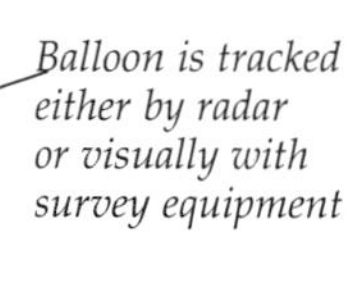

Balloon is tracked either by radar or visually with survey equipment

Tube for filling balloon with helium gas

Long line for supporting recording instruments

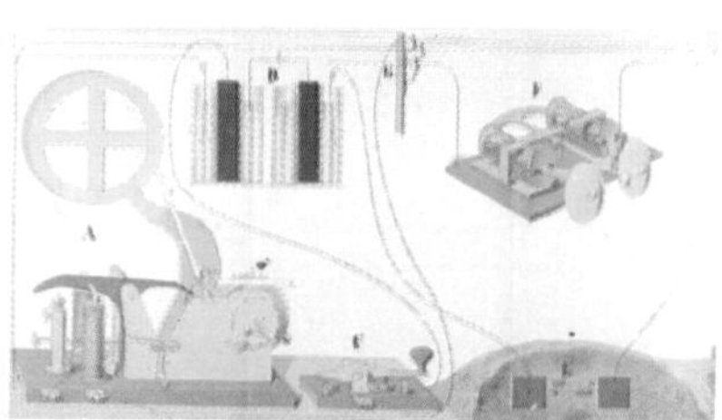

DATA COLLECTION

A crucial advance in accurate weather forecasting was Samuel Morse's invention of the telegraph in the 1840s. Complex messages were sent instantly over long distances through electric cables, by tapping out a coded sequence of short and long pauses, known as the Morse Code. Once a telegraph network was established, weather observations were sent back to a central bureau, giving a complete picture of a continent's weather.

Forecasting

EXPERIENCED WEATHER WATCHERS still predict local weather using simple instruments and careful observations of the skies. Larger-scale forecasting – the kind that provides daily radio and television reports – is a much more sophisticated and complex process. Every minute of the day and night, weather observations taken by weather stations, ships, satellites, balloons, and radar all around the world are swapped by means of a special Global Telecommunications System, or GTS. At major forecasting centers, all this data is continuously fed into powerful supercomputers, able to carry out millions of calculations a second. Meteorologists use this information to make short-range weather forecasts for the next 24 hours and draw up a special map, or synoptic chart, indicating air pressure, wind, cloud cover, temperature, and humidity. They can also make fairly accurate long-range forecasts for up to a week.

CHANGE OF AIR
French physicist Jean de Borda first showed that changes in air pressure are related to wind speed.

RAIN SCAN
Radar has proved invaluable in monitoring rainfall. Radar signals reflect any rain, hail, or snow within range, and the reflection's intensity shows how heavily rain is falling. Computer calculations then let meteorologists compile a map of rainfall intensity, as above.

HIGH DAYS
Fair weather, with blue skies and fluffy cumulus clouds (pp. 24–25), is often associated with high-pressure zones, or anticyclones.

Spiked and humped lines indicate occluded fronts, where cold fronts move beneath warm fronts and lift the warm air clear of the ground (pp. 32–35)

Spiked lines indicate a cold front, where cold air is pushing under warm

BAROGRAPH
Many fixed weather stations are equipped with a barograph to make a continuous record of changing air pressure. Like most barographs, this one is based around an aneroid barometer. Unlike mercury barometers (pp. 10–11), aneroid barometers have a drum that contains a vacuum sealed at a particular air pressure. As the air pressure changes, the drum expands and contracts. In a barograph, a pen attached to the lid of the drum draws the ups and downs continuously on a rotating sheet of graph paper.

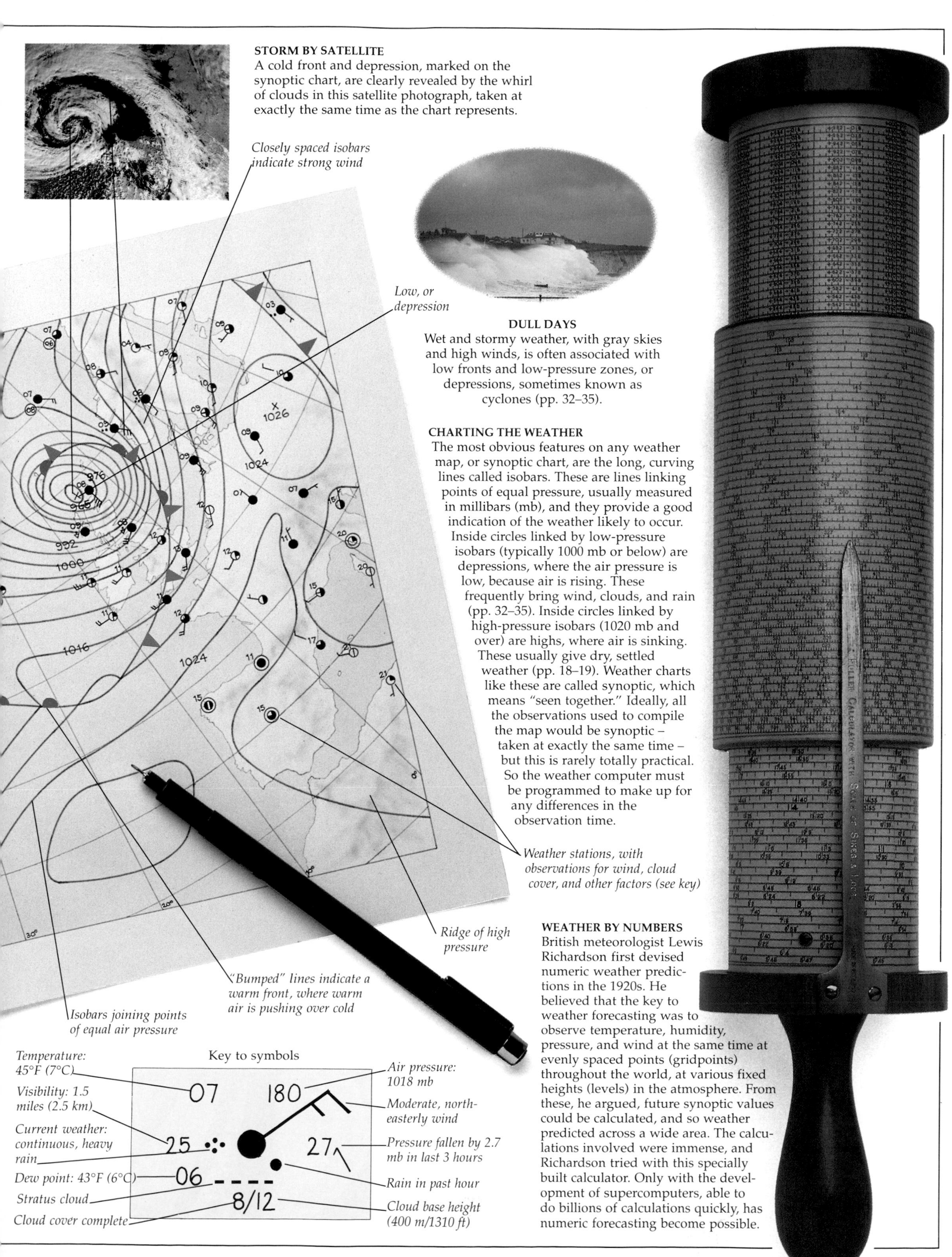

STORM BY SATELLITE
A cold front and depression, marked on the synoptic chart, are clearly revealed by the whirl of clouds in this satellite photograph, taken at exactly the same time as the chart represents.

DULL DAYS
Wet and stormy weather, with gray skies and high winds, is often associated with low fronts and low-pressure zones, or depressions, sometimes known as cyclones (pp. 32–35).

CHARTING THE WEATHER
The most obvious features on any weather map, or synoptic chart, are the long, curving lines called isobars. These are lines linking points of equal pressure, usually measured in millibars (mb), and they provide a good indication of the weather likely to occur. Inside circles linked by low-pressure isobars (typically 1000 mb or below) are depressions, where the air pressure is low, because air is rising. These frequently bring wind, clouds, and rain (pp. 32–35). Inside circles linked by high-pressure isobars (1020 mb and over) are highs, where air is sinking. These usually give dry, settled weather (pp. 18–19). Weather charts like these are called synoptic, which means "seen together." Ideally, all the observations used to compile the map would be synoptic – taken at exactly the same time – but this is rarely totally practical. So the weather computer must be programmed to make up for any differences in the observation time.

WEATHER BY NUMBERS
British meteorologist Lewis Richardson first devised numeric weather predictions in the 1920s. He believed that the key to weather forecasting was to observe temperature, humidity, pressure, and wind at the same time at evenly spaced points (gridpoints) throughout the world, at various fixed heights (levels) in the atmosphere. From these, he argued, future synoptic values could be calculated, and so weather predicted across a wide area. The calculations involved were immense, and Richardson tried with this specially built calculator. Only with the development of supercomputers, able to do billions of calculations quickly, has numeric forecasting become possible.

The power of the sun

A closeup view of the sun, showing a violent storm erupting at the surface

18th-century carved ivory pocket sundial

WITHOUT THE SUN, there would be no weather. Light from the sun is the energy which fuels the world's great weather machine. Sunshine, wind, rain, fog, snow, hail, thunder – every type of weather occurs because the heat of the sun keeps the atmosphere constantly in motion. But the power of the sun's rays to heat the air varies – across the world, through the day, and through the year. All these variations depend on the sun's height in the sky. When the sun is high in the sky, its rays strike the ground directly, and its heat is at a maximum. When it is low in the sky, the sun's rays strike the ground at an angle, and its heat is spread out over a wider area. It is largely because of these variations that we get hot weather and cold weather, hot places and cold places.

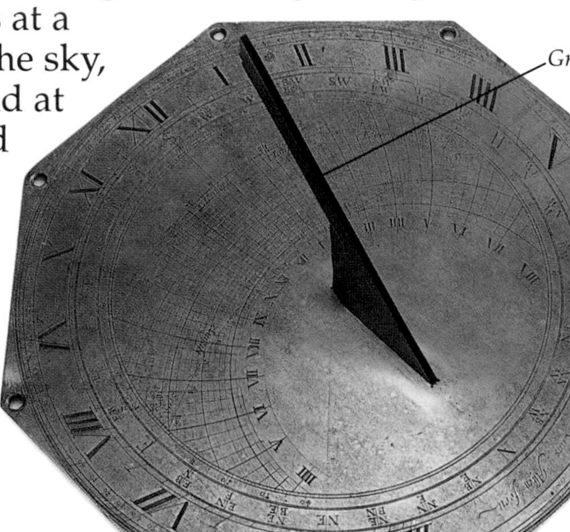

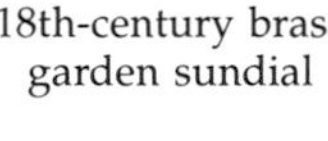

18th-century brass garden sundial

DAILY RHYTHMS *left and above*
The shadow cast by the sundial's needle, or gnomon, shifts as the sun moves through the sky from sunrise to sunset, indicating the time of day. In a similar manner, the sun's power to heat the air varies through the day – with profound effects upon the weather we experience (pp. 50–51).

HOT SPOTS
Deserts occur wherever the air is very dry and few clouds can form. The hottest deserts, like the Sahara, are in the tropics, but there are cold deserts in central Asia, far from the ocean.

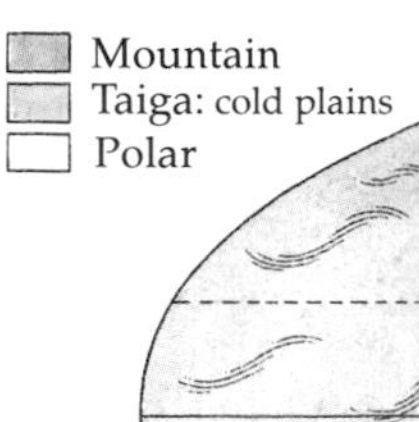

POLAR COLD
Vast areas of the Arctic and Antarctic, where it is always cold, are covered in a permanent sheet of ice, up to 985 ft (300 m) thick.

THE WORLD'S CLIMATES
Because the Earth's surface is curved, the sun's rays strike different parts at different angles, dividing the world into distinct climate zones, each with its own typical weather. (The "climate" of a place is its average weather.) The world's hottest places are in the tropics, straddling the equator, for here the sun is almost directly overhead at noon. The coldest places are at the poles, where even at noon the sun is so low in the sky that its power is spread out over a wide area. In between these extremes lie the temperate zones. Within these broad zones, climates vary considerably according to such factors as nearness to oceans and mountains, and height above sea level.

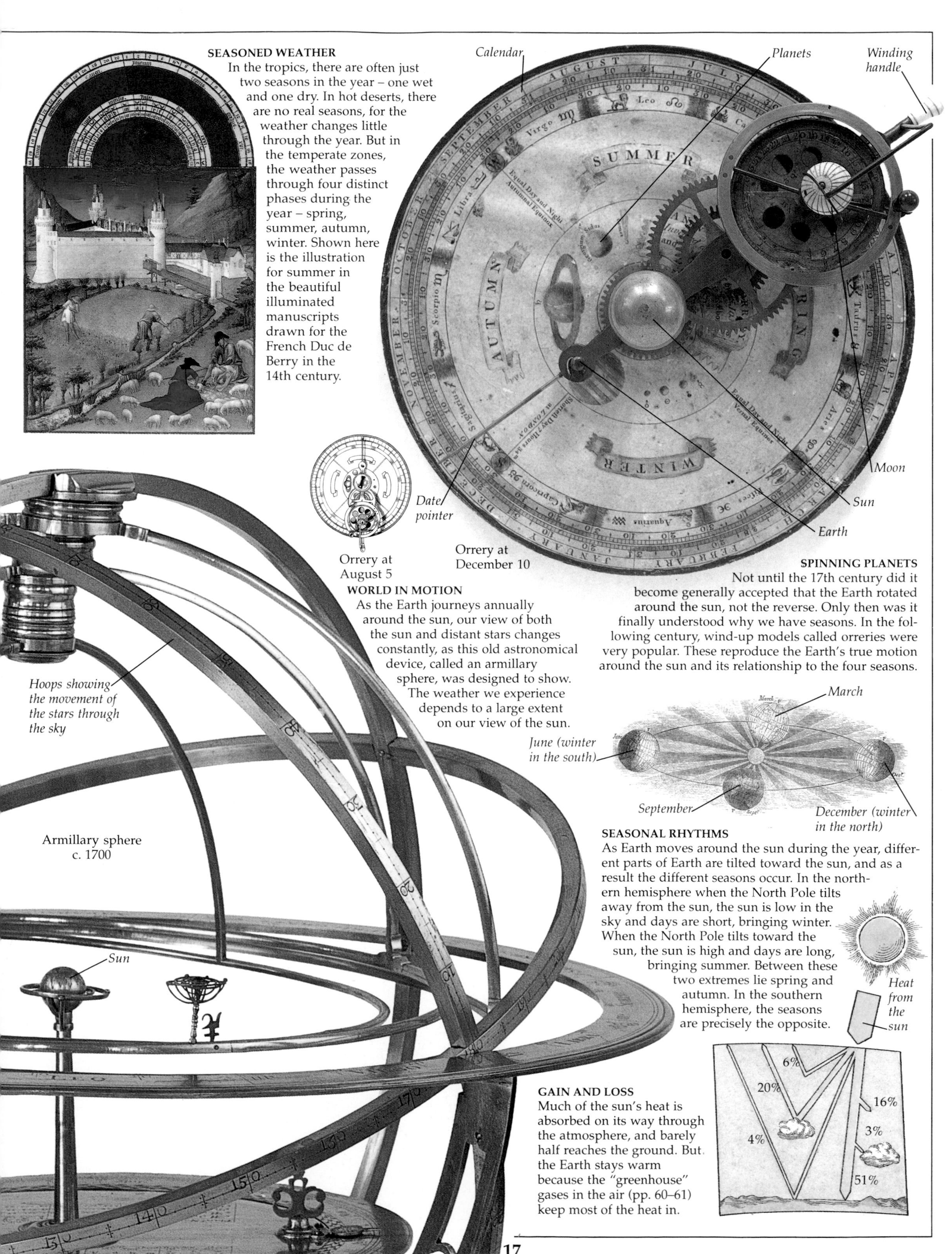

SEASONED WEATHER

In the tropics, there are often just two seasons in the year – one wet and one dry. In hot deserts, there are no real seasons, for the weather changes little through the year. But in the temperate zones, the weather passes through four distinct phases during the year – spring, summer, autumn, winter. Shown here is the illustration for summer in the beautiful illuminated manuscripts drawn for the French Duc de Berry in the 14th century.

Orrery at August 5

Orrery at December 10

SPINNING PLANETS

Not until the 17th century did it become generally accepted that the Earth rotated around the sun, not the reverse. Only then was it finally understood why we have seasons. In the following century, wind-up models called orreries were very popular. These reproduce the Earth's true motion around the sun and its relationship to the four seasons.

WORLD IN MOTION

As the Earth journeys annually around the sun, our view of both the sun and distant stars changes constantly, as this old astronomical device, called an armillary sphere, was designed to show. The weather we experience depends to a large extent on our view of the sun.

Armillary sphere c. 1700

SEASONAL RHYTHMS

As Earth moves around the sun during the year, different parts of Earth are tilted toward the sun, and as a result the different seasons occur. In the northern hemisphere when the North Pole tilts away from the sun, the sun is low in the sky and days are short, bringing winter. When the North Pole tilts toward the sun, the sun is high and days are long, bringing summer. Between these two extremes lie spring and autumn. In the southern hemisphere, the seasons are precisely the opposite.

GAIN AND LOSS

Much of the sun's heat is absorbed on its way through the atmosphere, and barely half reaches the ground. But the Earth stays warm because the "greenhouse" gases in the air (pp. 60–61) keep most of the heat in.

A sunny day

OVER MUCH OF THE WORLD, sunny weather and nearly cloudless skies are common, especially in summer. Indeed, in the eastern Sahara Desert, the sun is covered by clouds for fewer than 100 hours of the year. Sunny weather is actually the most stable, persistent kind of weather, and a day that starts sunny and cloudless is likely to stay that way. Clouds form only when there is enough moisture in the air – and enough movement to carry the moisture high into the atmosphere. If the air is both dry and calm, clouds will not form, nor will they be blown in from elsewhere. This is why sunny weather is often associated with high atmospheric pressure (pp. 14–15), where the air is slowly sinking and virtually still. In summer, high pressure can persist for a long time – as the sinking air pushes out any new influences – and the weather remains warm and sunny for days on end.

The hottest place in the world is Dallol in Ethiopia (East Africa), where annual temperatures average 94°F (34.4°C).

SUN GOD
So important was reliable sunshine in ancient times – not only for heat and light but for ripening crops – that many early civilizations worshiped the sun. The Aztecs of Mexico, for example, built vast temples to the sun god Tonatuich, and made many bloody sacrifices, both animal and human, to persuade him to shine brightly on them.

GROWING LIGHT
Green plants need plenty of sunshine, for all their energy for growth comes directly from the sun. Cells in their leaves contain chlorophyll, which converts sunlight into chemical energy by photosynthesis.

SOLAR POWER
Nearly all our energy comes from the sun. Solar cells let us tap this energy directly, using light-sensitive crystals to convert sunshine into electricity. Solar power is only practical in places with plenty of sunshine.

BURNING RECORD
Meteorologists usually record hours of sunshine on a simple device called a Campbell-Stokes sunshine recorder. This has a glass ball to focus the sun's rays onto a strip of paper so that they burn it. As the sun moves around during the day, so do the scorch marks on the paper, giving a complete scorch-mark record of the day's sunshine. This early recorder (viewed from above) was made by Irish physicist George Stokes in 1881.

Image of sun reflected in glass orb

Burn marks on card

BLUE SKY
In summer, sunny days tend to be hot, as there are few clouds in the way to block out the sun's rays – clouds can soak up more than 80 percent of the sun's heat on a cloudy day. But without clouds to trap heat rising from the ground, temperatures can often drop rapidly after sunset. Indeed, in winter sunny weather usually brings foggy mornings and frosty nights. Clear, blue skies may look uninteresting at first sight, but there is often plenty going on, especially when the atmosphere is humid (pp. 50–51) or dusty.

Wisps of high cirrus cloud, made entirely of ice. These may be the remnants of a vanished storm cloud, since ice vaporizes more slowly than water. But they could signal the onset of a warm front (pp. 32–33)

Remnants of contrails

Contrails left in the wake of jet planes, especially in cold, dry air. Made of ice, like cirrus clouds, contrails form when the hot gases that shoot out behind the jet hit cool air and rise rapidly. As they rise, they expand and cool so sharply that water droplets soon condense and then freeze

Small, short-lived, fluffy cumulus clouds may be formed here and there by rising warm air currents

Low-level haze, especially over urban areas. Winds may be too light to disperse smoke and dust, and if the pressure is high, a temperature inversion may trap water vapor and pollutants in a layer just above the ground (pp. 48–49)

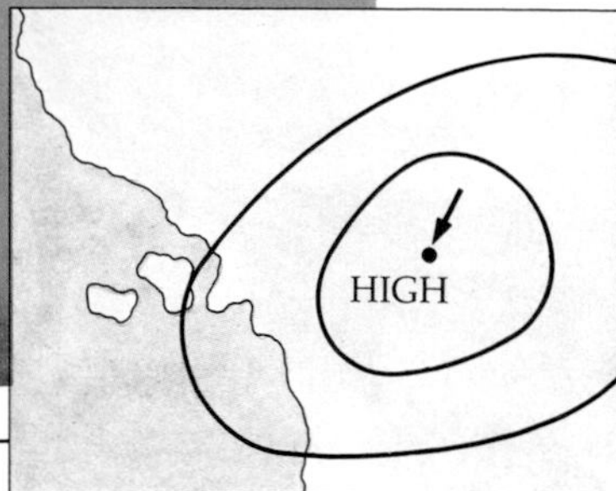

Frost and ice

KEEPING THE COLD OUT
In some parts of the world, frosty nights are characterized by the malevolent, spiky "Jack Frost," who leaves his icy finger marks on every window pane.

WHEN A CALM, CLEAR, DRY NIGHT follows a cold winter's day, a sharp frost may well descend on many places by morning. Temperatures rarely climb high in winter, when the sun is low in the sky during the day and the nights are long. If the night sky is clear, too, then any heat retained in the ground can flow away quickly, allowing temperatures to drop quickly. Frosts are rare but by no means unheard of in the tropics – and almost continuous toward the poles. At Vostok, in Antarctica, temperatures average a bitter -72°F (-57.8°C). In the mid-latitudes (pp. 32–33), frosts occur whenever the conditions are right, more often inland than near the coast, because the sea tends to retain heat longer than the land.

1020 mb

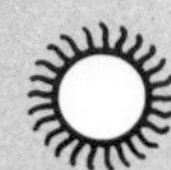
Full sun

Little wind

The low temperatures near the ground that bring a frost can also create fog (pp. 48–49). The moisture condenses in the cold air and hangs there, because there is little wind to disperse it. If the fog coats things with ice, it is called freezing fog

Thick coating of rime, a white ice formed when an icy wind blows over leaves, branches, and other surfaces. Temperatures usually have to be lower for rime than for hoar frost

Hoar frost coats freezing cold surfaces such as soil and metal with ice crystals

ICING UP
High in the atmosphere, air temperatures are always below freezing, and the wings of high-flying airplanes can easily become coated with ice. This drastically affects their performance. All jet airliners now have de-icing equipment.

HOAR THORNS
When water vapor touches a very cold surface, it can freeze instantly, leaving spiky needles of hoar frost on leaves and branches – and also on cars, for their metal bodies get very cold. Hoar frost tends to occur when the air temperature is around 32°F (0°C), and the ground is much colder – but the air must be moist to create the ice crystals.

COLD FRAME
Frost can create beautiful patterns of ice crystals. If the weather is especially severe, delicate outlines of "fern frost" may appear on the inside of windows. First, dew forms on the cold glass. Then, as some dewdrops cool below freezing point, they turn into ice crystals, and soon more ice crystals form.

FROZEN ARCH
Arctic and Antarctic temperatures are always below freezing, and ice can last hundreds of years. Sometimes vast chunks of ice, or icebergs, break off polar glaciers and float out to sea. They float because water becomes lighter and less dense when it freezes.

Even though there is a mist near the ground, the sky above is clear, allowing heat to escape during the night

Frost is white because the crystals contain air

ICY COATING *(above)*
When the conditions are cold enough, moisture from the air freezes, leaving the ground, leaves, branches, and many other surfaces coated with a thin layer of ice crystals. Sometimes, though, frost can occur because heat is radiated from the ground on clear nights. Spring and autumn frosts often happen this way. In midwinter, though, a chill polar wind may be enough to bring frost.

ICE HOUSE
Very low temperatures can produce spectacular ice effects. Most icicles form when cold nights freeze drips of melting snow. This house in Chicago, Illinois, got its remarkable coat of ice when firefighters turned their hoses on it to put out a fire – on the coldest night in the city's history, when temperatures plunged to -26°F (-32°C) on January 10, 1982.

MARKET ON ICE
In the early 1800s, the weather tended to be much colder than today. Frosts could be so hard that even the Thames River in London froze solid. The last "frost fair" held on the ice was in 1814, before the weather began to warm up.

Water in the air

EVEN ON THE SUNNIEST DAY, the horizon often shimmers indistinctly in a haze, and distant hills look soft and gray. Some haze is dust and pollution, but most is simply moisture in the air. Even over the hottest deserts, the atmosphere contains some moisture. Like a dry sponge, the air continually soaks up water that evaporates from oceans, lakes, and rivers, and transpires from trees, grass, and other plants. Most of the moisture is water vapor, a gas mixed invisibly into the air. When it cools enough, the moisture condenses into tiny droplets of water, forming the clouds, mist, and haze that continually girdle the Earth. Water vapor will form water droplets only if the air contains plenty of dust, smoke, and salt particles, called condensation nuclei, for it to condense on to. If the air is very pure, there will not be enough nuclei, so clouds and mist will not form.

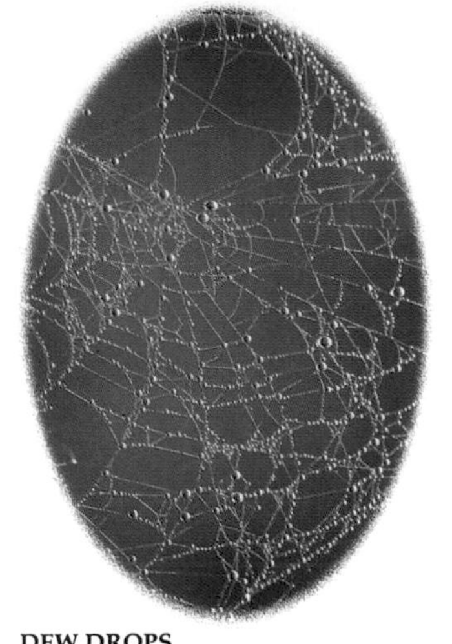

DEW DROPS
Moisture condenses as air cools because the cooler the air is, the less water vapor it can hold. So as it cools down, air becomes nearer saturation – that is, the limit it can hold. Once it reaches this limit, called the dew point, water vapor condenses into droplets. After a cold night, dew drops can be seen sparkling on grass and spiders' webs.

Scale shows humidity

Human hair stretches in moist air and contracts in dry air

Hair hygrometer

WET HAIR
The moisture content of the air, called humidity, can be measured using a hair hygrometer. Meteorologists need to know how much water there is in the air, in proportion to the most water it can hold at that temperature and pressure. This is called relative humidity.

When the water level in the spout is high, pressure is low, and storms can be expected

Closed glass bulb

When working, the level of water in the weather glass would have been much higher

STORM GLASS
Like mercury in a barometer, water levels can be used to monitor air pressure. Though inaccurate, "weather glasses" like this were much cheaper to make than real mercury barometers, and used to be popular on small boats.

WEATHER HOUSE
Before weather forecasting was common, weather houses like this were popular. Actually, they are hair hygrometers. When the air is moist, a hair inside the house expands and lets the man come out of the door. If the air is dry, the hair shrinks, pulling the man in and letting the woman pop out.

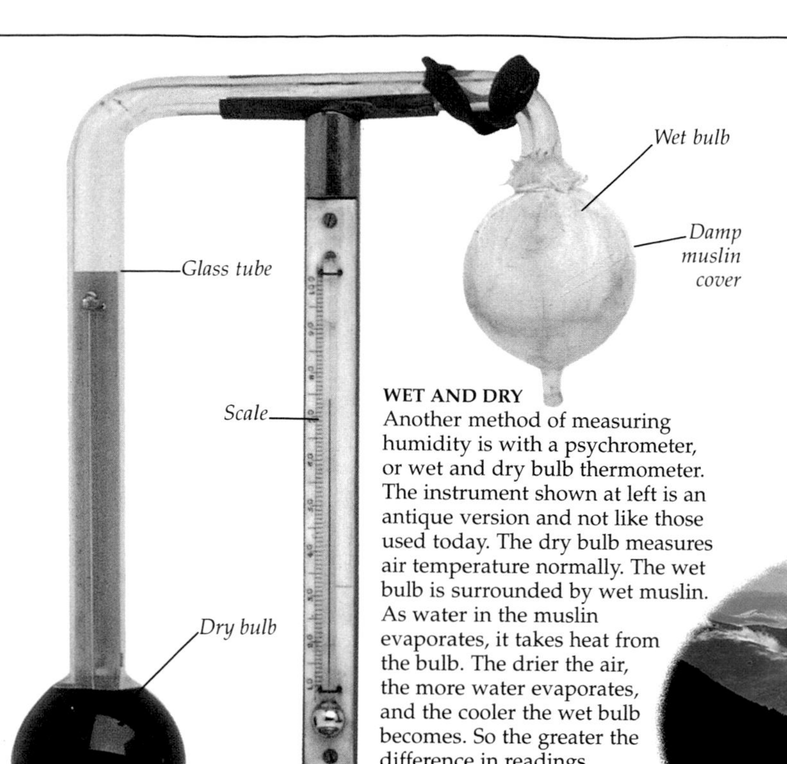

WET AND DRY
Another method of measuring humidity is with a psychrometer, or wet and dry bulb thermometer. The instrument shown at left is an antique version and not like those used today. The dry bulb measures air temperature normally. The wet bulb is surrounded by wet muslin. As water in the muslin evaporates, it takes heat from the bulb. The drier the air, the more water evaporates, and the cooler the wet bulb becomes. So the greater the difference in readings between the wet and dry bulbs, the lower the humidity.

SMALL MEASURES
This tiny pocket hygrometer – less than 1.5 in (4 cm) in diameter – uses human hair to work the needle and is surprisingly accurate. Instruments like this used to be very popular with hikers, who wanted to predict a shower.

MISTY MOUNTAINS
At night, the ground cools down gradually, and so cools the air above it. If the air temperature drops below its dew point, it becomes saturated, and water droplets condense into the air to form a mist. In mountain areas (pp. 52–53), mist will often gather in the valleys in the morning because cold air flows downhill in the night and settles there.

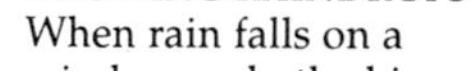

WATER VISION
If it were not for the moisture in the air, we could nearly always see into the distance much more clearly. Fog and mist cut down visibility dramatically, but even on apparently clear days, there is often a slight haze in the air, making distant hills look pale and indistinct.

GROWING RAINDROPS
When rain falls on a window, only the biggest drops run down the pane. Unless a raindrop is big to start with, a phenomenon known as surface tension will hold it on the glass until another drop falls in the same place. Then the tension will be broken, and the drops will run down the pane in rivulets. In the same way, tiny droplets of water in a cloud will only start to fall as rain once they are large and heavy enough to overcome air resistance.

DAMP TRADE
Many activities, such as silk-making in China, depend upon the humidity of the air. If the air is not damp enough, the caterpillars will not spin the thread properly.

The birth of a cloud

LOOK INTO THE SKY ON A FAIR DAY, when fleecy, "cotton-ball" clouds are scudding overhead. Watch carefully for a while and you will see the clouds constantly changing in shape and size. Every so often, new clouds appear out of the blue, curling and growing like cotton candy. Others shrink and vanish into nothing, especially late in the day as the ground grows cooler. Short-lived clouds like these, called cumulus, or "heap" clouds, form because the sun heats the ground unevenly. In some places this creates bubbles of warm air that drift upward through the cooler air around. As they rise, the bubbles cool, until, high in the air, water vapor condenses to form a cloud. Bubbles, or convection cells, like these rarely last for more than 20 minutes. Often, half a dozen new cells bubble up in the same place and the resulting cloud can last for an hour or so. A few clouds may build up so much that an isolated shower of rain will fall.

Occasionally, when the air is moist and the sun hot, fleecy cumulus clouds grow enough to create their own internal air currents, and then something more ominous starts to happen. The cloud billows higher into the atmosphere, and may turn into a huge thundercloud, lasting for about nine hours, before releasing its large load of moisture in a terrific downpour (pp. 36–37).

HOT AIR
As air heats up, it expands and becomes lighter than the surrounding cool air, and so it rises. The Montgolfier brothers used this principle when they filled a balloon with hot air heated by a fire in a huge kettle beneath it to make the first-ever manned flight over Paris in 1783.

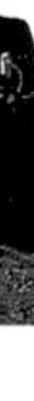

STEAM CLOUDS
Clouds form in the sky in much the same way that clouds of steam billow from a steam engine's funnel. As hot, moist air escapes from the funnel, the air expands and becomes cooler, until it is so cold that any moisture condenses into tiny water droplets. So a bubble of rising, warm air expands and cools until water vapor condenses to form clouds.

Early clouds often disappear, evaporating into the drier surrounding air

1 SMALL BEGINNINGS
It takes some time for the sun to heat the ground, so the first clouds are very small.

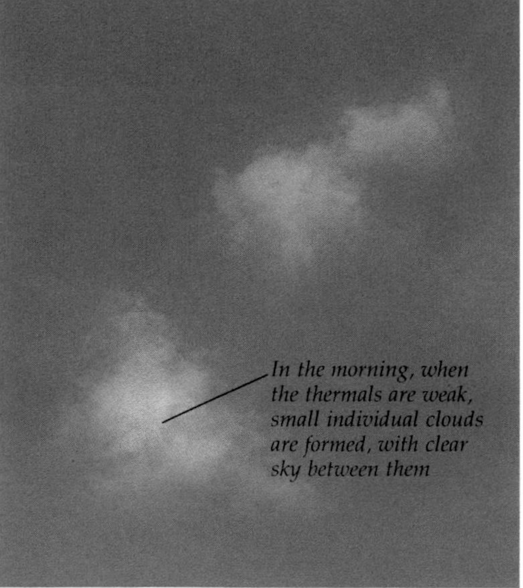

In the morning, when the thermals are weak, small individual clouds are formed, with clear sky between them

2 NEW BUBBLES
The same areas of the ground often remain hottest during the day, so warm air continues to bubble up in the same places. Sometimes, the clouds formed by these bubbles will drift away on the wind, and another will take its place, creating "streets," or lines, of clouds for many miles downwind.

Clouds often lean downwind, because the air is moving faster at higher levels than lower down toward the surface

3 BUILDING CLOUDS
Clouds will evaporate and disappear only if the surrounding air is dry, so any increase in moisture means that they evaporate more slowly. They will last longer as the day goes by, because rising air will continue to bring in new moisture.

Thermals

Bubbles of warm air, or thermals, form over hot spots on the ground, such as at an airport. Because the bubble is warmer, it expands, becoming less dense than the surrounding air. Drifting up into the sky, it expands farther as air becomes thinner and pressure drops. As it expands, it cools down until at a certain height – the condensation level – it is so cool that the moisture it contains condenses.

ELK'S BREATH

The warm, moist breath of a mammal is usually invisible – unless the air is so cold that moisture in the animal's breath condenses into droplets and then turns into tiny clouds.

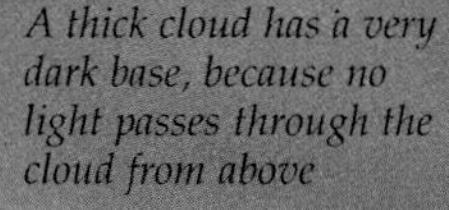

A thick cloud has a very dark base, because no light passes through the cloud from above

5 HIGH FLIERS

The movement of air inside cumulus clouds often becomes organized into "cells," with strong updrafts and downdrafts quite close to one another. Pilots try to avoid flying through large cumulus clouds, because the sudden changes between rising and falling air cause a very bumpy ride, and passengers have to wear seatbelts. The cloud that is shown in these pictures has now grown very large. If it grew even larger, some of the water vapor might turn to ice, which would start the formation of raindrops.

Clouds appear brilliantly white in sunshine, because the tiny water droplets reflect light extremely well

4 UP, UP, AND AWAY

As the day heats up, more thermals drift up from the surface. One may arrive so close behind another that a single cloud is created. Moist air around the first thermal helps the second to grow higher before it too starts to disappear. Each cloud contains several thermals at different stages of development.

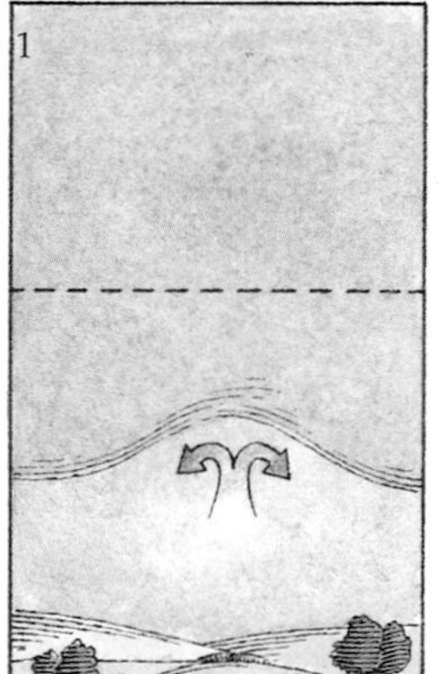

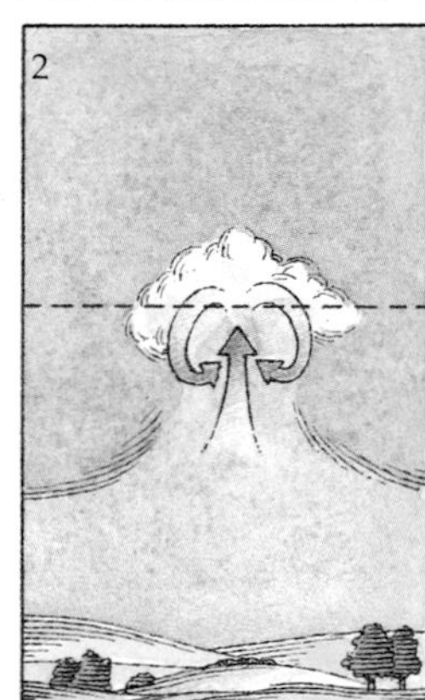

A CLOUD FORMS

Clouds form whenever there is enough moisture in the air, and whenever moist air is lifted high enough into the air to cool and condense (1). On a clear day, the sun heats the ground, sending up bubbles of rising warm air wherever the ground becomes warmest (2). Fleecy cumulus clouds will appear in the sky and disappear when these bubbles no longer form (3).

ARTIFICIAL CLOUDS

Not all clouds are natural ones. Inside power-station cooling towers, the large quantities of water at a low temperature produce enormous volumes of very moist, slightly warm air, which often condenses immediately above the towers into low, "artificial" cumulus clouds.

A cloudy day

CLOUDY SKIES ARE RARE OVER DRY DESERTS. But in more humid areas, the weather may stay dull and overcast for days on end. Sometimes, fluffy, short-lived cumulus clouds (pp. 28–29) heap up enough to form a dense bank, shutting out the sun. More often, though, persistently cloudy skies are associated with layered, or stratus, clouds. Clouds like these build up gradually over a wide area when a warm, moist wind meets colder air. As this warm air rides slowly up over cold air, moisture steadily condenses from the air as it cools – creating a vast blanket of cloud that can be several hundred feet thick and stretch for hundreds of miles.

MEASURING CLOUD HEIGHT
The Victorians calculated the height of clouds by using cameras and giant tripods, but meteorologists nowadays use laser beams pointed at the base of the cloud to judge its height. Cloud cover, however, is worked out visually, by estimating roughly what proportion of the sky is obscured by the cloud directly overhead – usually in tenths or eighths.

THREE KINDS OF CLOUD
On some cloudy days, nothing but a thin blanket of low stratus is visible. On other days, many kinds of clouds may be seen at different heights in the sky. Thin sheets of stratus may not be enough to stop warm updrafts of air, or thermals, from developing and cumulus clouds from growing (pp. 24–25), especially if the sun is strong. In this picture, taken near mountains close to a weak cold front (pp. 34–35), there are not only stratus and cumulus, but also a third type, called lenticular clouds, formed by waves in the wind in the lee of mountains (pp. 54–55).

Small cumulus clouds are unlikely to give much rain – although there might be light showers later in the day

Stratus cloud

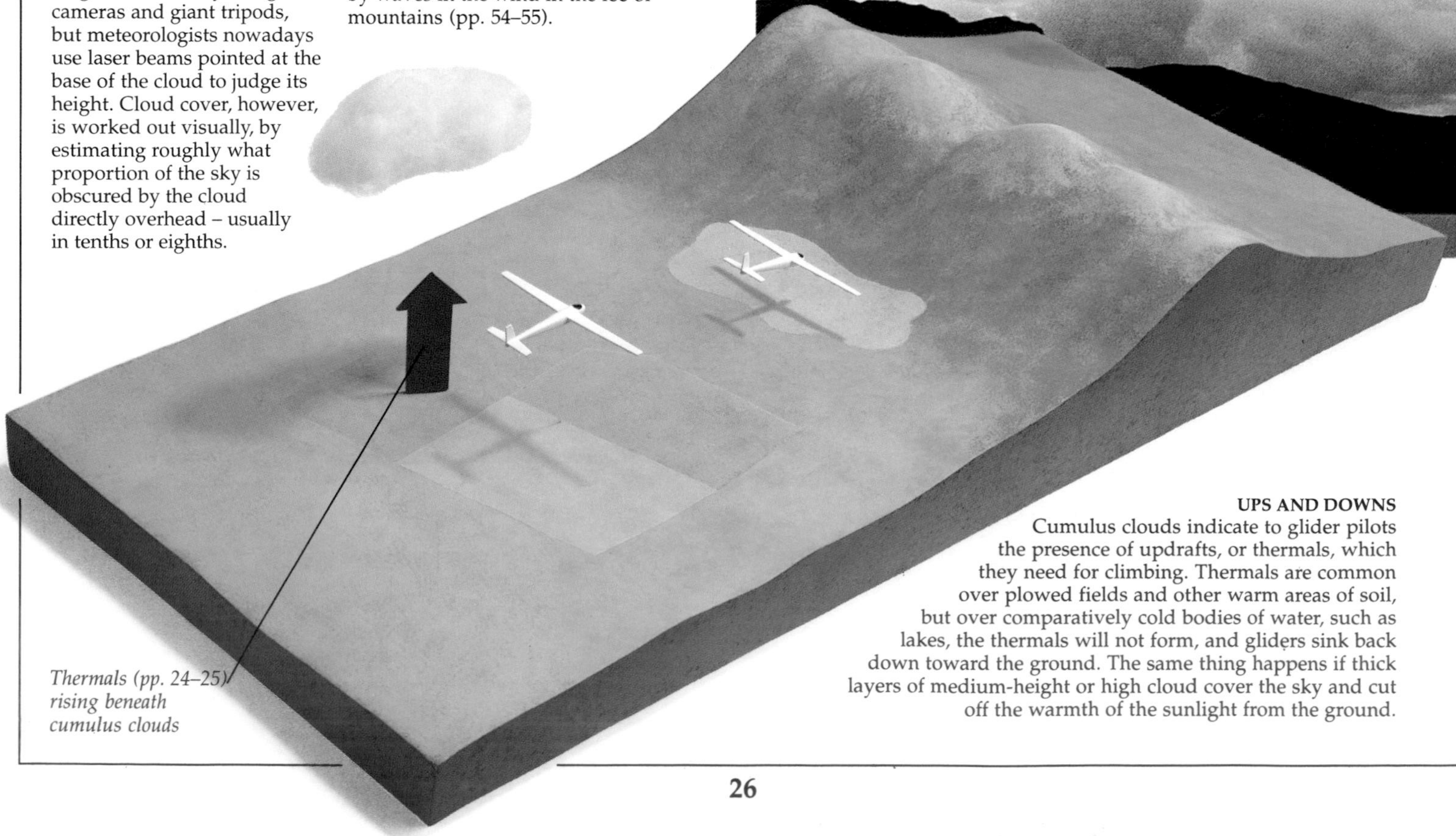

UPS AND DOWNS
Cumulus clouds indicate to glider pilots the presence of updrafts, or thermals, which they need for climbing. Thermals are common over plowed fields and other warm areas of soil, but over comparatively cold bodies of water, such as lakes, the thermals will not form, and gliders sink back down toward the ground. The same thing happens if thick layers of medium-height or high cloud cover the sky and cut off the warmth of the sunlight from the ground.

Thermals (pp. 24–25) rising beneath cumulus clouds

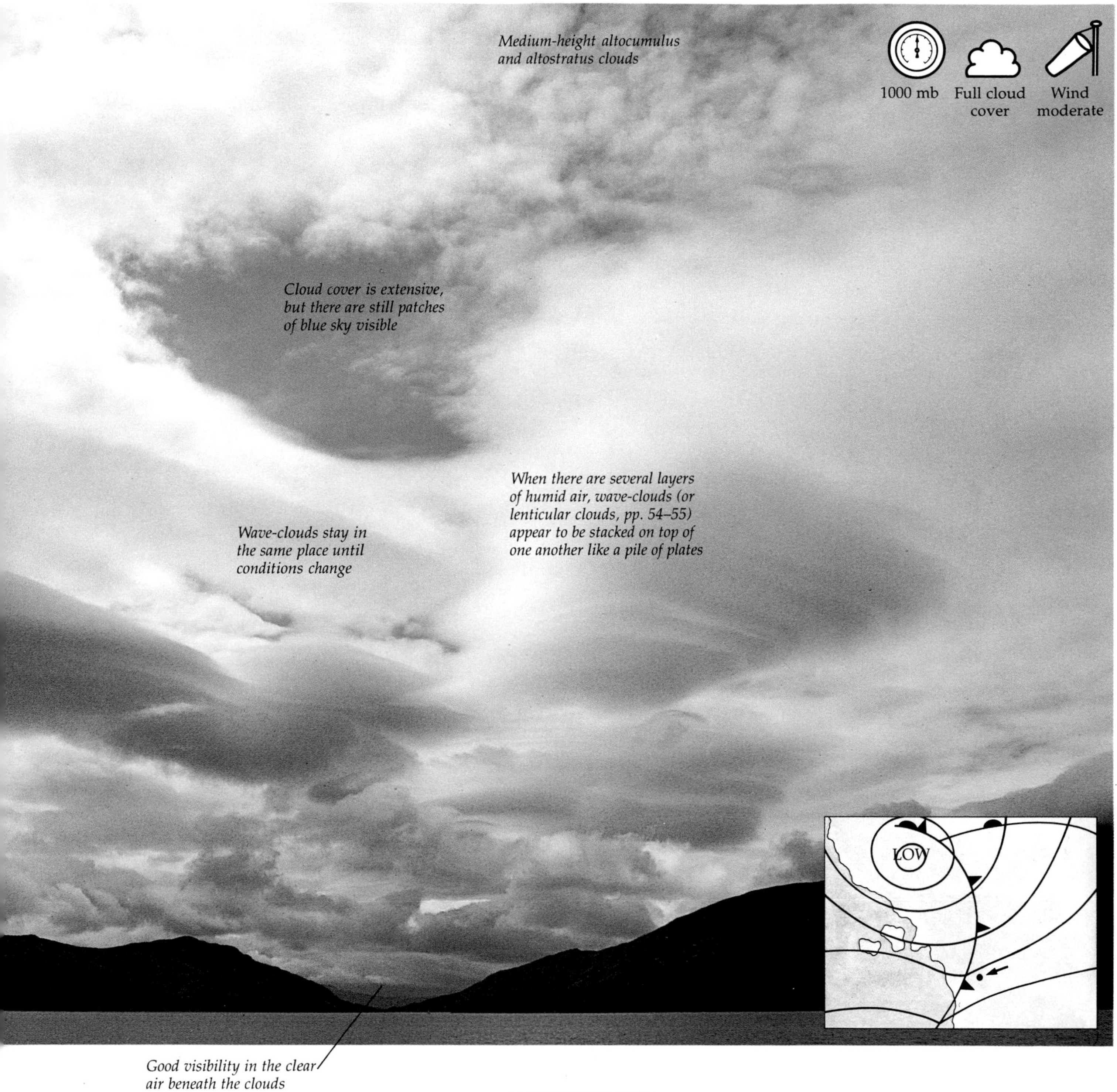

Medium-height altocumulus and altostratus clouds

1000 mb

Full cloud cover

Wind moderate

Cloud cover is extensive, but there are still patches of blue sky visible

When there are several layers of humid air, wave-clouds (or lenticular clouds, pp. 54–55) appear to be stacked on top of one another like a pile of plates

Wave-clouds stay in the same place until conditions change

LOW

Good visibility in the clear air beneath the clouds

SMOOTH OR LUMPY

In *The Beauty of the Heavens* (London, 1845), the painter Charles F. Blunt depicted two main groups of clouds: cumulus (detail, left), which are heaped clouds formed by the rise of individual bubbles of air (pp. 24–25); and cirrostratus (detail, right), where whole layers of air are forced to rise, for example at a front (pp. 32–33), forming widespread sheets of cloud.

Clouds of all kinds

CLOUDS FLOAT ACROSS THE SKY in all sorts of shapes, sizes, and colors, from white, wispy mares' tails to towering, lead-gray thunder-clouds. There is such an amazing variety of clouds that no single system of classification could ever do them justice – yet none has been found to improve the system devised by the English pharmacist Luke Howard in 1803. Howard identified ten distinct categories of cloud, all of which are variations on three basic cloud forms – puffy cumulus clouds, stratus clouds forming in layers, and feathery cirrus clouds. This system proved so simple and effective that it is still used by meteorologists today.

LUKE HOWARD (1772–1864)
A keen amateur meteorologist, Howard devised his system by regularly observing clouds and analyzing their shapes and heights.

FLYING SAUCERS
Lenticular clouds (pp. 54–55), so-called because they look like lenses, always form in the lee of mountains.

TRANSLUCENT CLOUD
Altostratus are high, thin sheets of cloud that can often completely cover the sky, so that the sun looks as if it is seen through misty glass. At a warm front (pp. 32–33), lower, thicker, nimbostratus, rain clouds normally follow.

Temperature here -40°F (-40°C)

Cloud spreads out at the top where the air stops rising at the tropopause (pp. 6–7). This is sometimes called the anvil, because it is shaped like an old blacksmith's anvil

FLEECY CLOUDS *left*
Altocumulus are puffs and rolls of cloud, visible at medium heights. Unlike the higher, smaller cirrocumulus, they often have dark, shadowed sides.

A GRAY BLANKET *left*
Stratus is a vast, dull type of cloud that hangs low over the ground and may give a damp drizzle, but no real rain. Higher up, on hills or even from tall buildings, stratus simply appears as fog.

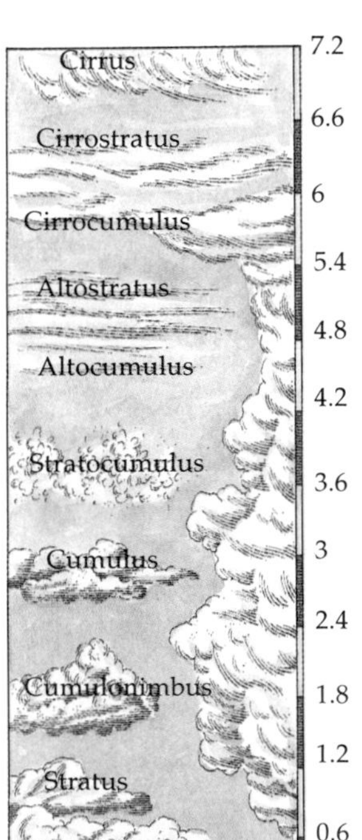

CLOUD HEIGHTS
Cirrus-type clouds, including cirrocumulus and cirrostratus, form at the top of the troposphere, where it is coldest. Altostratus and altocumulus are found at medium heights; stratocumulus, stratus, nimbostratus, and cumulus, closer to the ground (pp. 6–7). Cumulonimbus may reach up through the whole troposphere.

Temperature here 32° F (0° C)

MARES' TAILS
Cirrus clouds form high in the sky where the atmosphere is so cold that they are made entirely from ice crystals. Strong winds blow the crystals into wispy "mares' tails."

TRAILING VIRGA
Cumulus clouds sometimes let rain or ice crystals fall into drier, slower-moving layers of air. The streaks that result, known as virga, evaporate before they reach the ground, and from below look as if they are vanishing into thin air.

AN ICY VEIL
Cirrostratus occur when cirrus clouds spread into a thin, milky sheet. Here the sun appears very bright and may have one or more colored rings, or haloes, around it and, occasionally, brilliant "mock suns" (pp. 58–59).

Mainly ice crystals

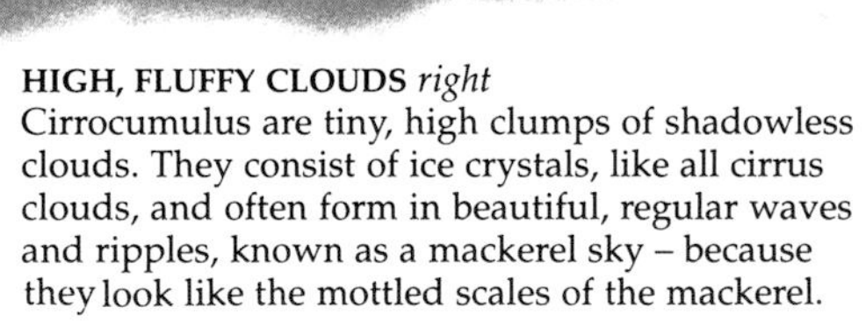

HIGH, FLUFFY CLOUDS *right*
Cirrocumulus are tiny, high clumps of shadowless clouds. They consist of ice crystals, like all cirrus clouds, and often form in beautiful, regular waves and ripples, known as a mackerel sky – because they look like the mottled scales of the mackerel.

Cloud moves from left to right

Strong updrafts carry billows of cloud high into the atmosphere

A LAYER OF CUMULUS
Stratocumulus often form when the tops of cumulus clouds rise and spread out sideways into broad sheets. Viewed from an airplane, they look like a waving blanket of rolls and pancakes of cloud, with narrow breaks sometimes showing a glimpse of the ground.

Mixture of ice crystals and water

SHOWER CLOUDS *left*
Bigger and darker than cumulus, cumulonimbus usually bring rain showers – nimbus means "rain" in Latin. Sometimes they grow huge and unleash sudden, gigantic thunderstorms.

Violent updrafts and downdrafts in the front wall of cloud create hailstones (pp. 36–37)

Mainly water droplets

Air drawn in here

CAULIFLOWER CLOUDS
Cumulus clouds often mass together and grow upward with dense, white heads, looking just like cauliflowers. If they keep on growing, they may become rain-bearing cumulonimbus.

A rainy day

SOMBER, SLATE-GRAY CLOUDS are a sure sign of imminent rain. They are dark because they are so deep and full of water that no sunlight penetrates them. The heaviest downpours fall from the deepest, darkest clouds, which have all the height needed for raindrops to develop properly. In the tropics, huge cumulonimbus clouds often tower 9 miles (15 km) into the sky, and can occasionally unleash a deluge of 3 ft (0.9 m) in an afternoon. The duration and intensity of showers varies greatly. Blankets of lighter, thinner nimbostratus clouds tend to give slower, steadier rain that may last for hours, and even days, on end. Low stratus can envelop you in a persistent drizzle that is little more than a mist.

POURING PETS
There have been reports of tornado-like updrafts that bring heavy rain and have also caused creatures as large as frogs and fish to be lifted up into the air. As for the old saying, *"It's raining cats and dogs,"* this may be partly based on the ancient Chinese spirits for rain and wind, which were sometimes depicted as a cat and a dog.

SOAKING
Meteorologists describe rain as light if less than 1/48 in (0.5 mm) falls in an hour, and heavy if more than 1/6 in (4 mm) falls. In the mid-latitudes (pp. 32–33), heavy rain does not usually last more than an hour. Only moderate or light rain persists. Even the worst downpours are rarely heavier than those experienced almost every day in many tropical areas.

Heavy rain can saturate the air beneath the cloud so that further condensation takes place into cloud beneath the main base

CLOUDBURST *right*
A cloudburst happens when a cumulonimbus dies – its cold downdrafts overwhelm the warm updrafts that sustain it – and releases all its moisture at once. Clouds like this often form along cold fronts (pp. 34–35) and in their wake.

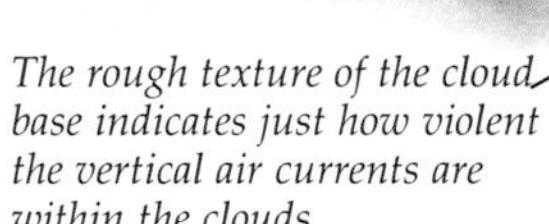

The rough texture of the cloud base indicates just how violent the vertical air currents are within the clouds

OUT ON THE TILES
Exceptionally heavy rain can bring flooding to low-lying districts – especially when the rain comes after a long, dry period. After a drought, the soil can be baked so hard that rain water cannot drain away properly. Instead, it runs off across the surface.

Water runs down funnel and is collected in the cylinder below

DEEP WATER *right*
Rainfall is usually measured by recording the depth of water that collects in a rain gauge. A rain gauge is simply a drum about 20 in (50 cm) tall set on the ground just high enough to avoid splashes. Rain water is caught in the funnel at the top and runs down into a measuring cylinder.

Rolls of cloud develop as falling rain sweeps colder air down toward the ground, forcing warm air upward to start off another cloud

Rain falling from the base of the cloud

This man with his geese (from a Japanese woodcut) knows that rain is on the way, and has his umbrella ready

STORM WATERS
Some of the worst floods are caused not by rain but by storms at sea. Huge waves form and the surging waters swamp coastal regions (pp. 44–45).

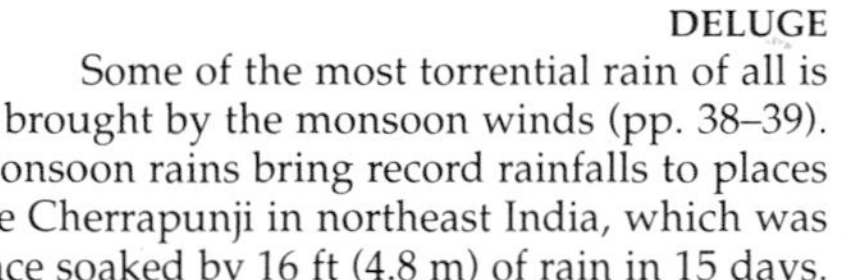

DELUGE
Some of the most torrential rain of all is brought by the monsoon winds (pp. 38–39). Monsoon rains bring record rainfalls to places like Cherrapunji in northeast India, which was once soaked by 16 ft (4.8 m) of rain in 15 days.

Fronts and lows

In the mid-latitudes of the world – between the tropics and the polar regions – much of the year's foulest, most unpleasant weather comes from great, spiraling weather systems which are called depressions or lows. Particularly in winter, "families" of depressions whirl in from the west like giant pinwheels, bringing with them cooler weather, cloudy skies, blustery winds, rain, and snow. A big depression may be hundreds of miles wide, but it sweeps quickly across the countryside, usually passing overhead in less than 24 hours, bringing a now well known sequence of weather.

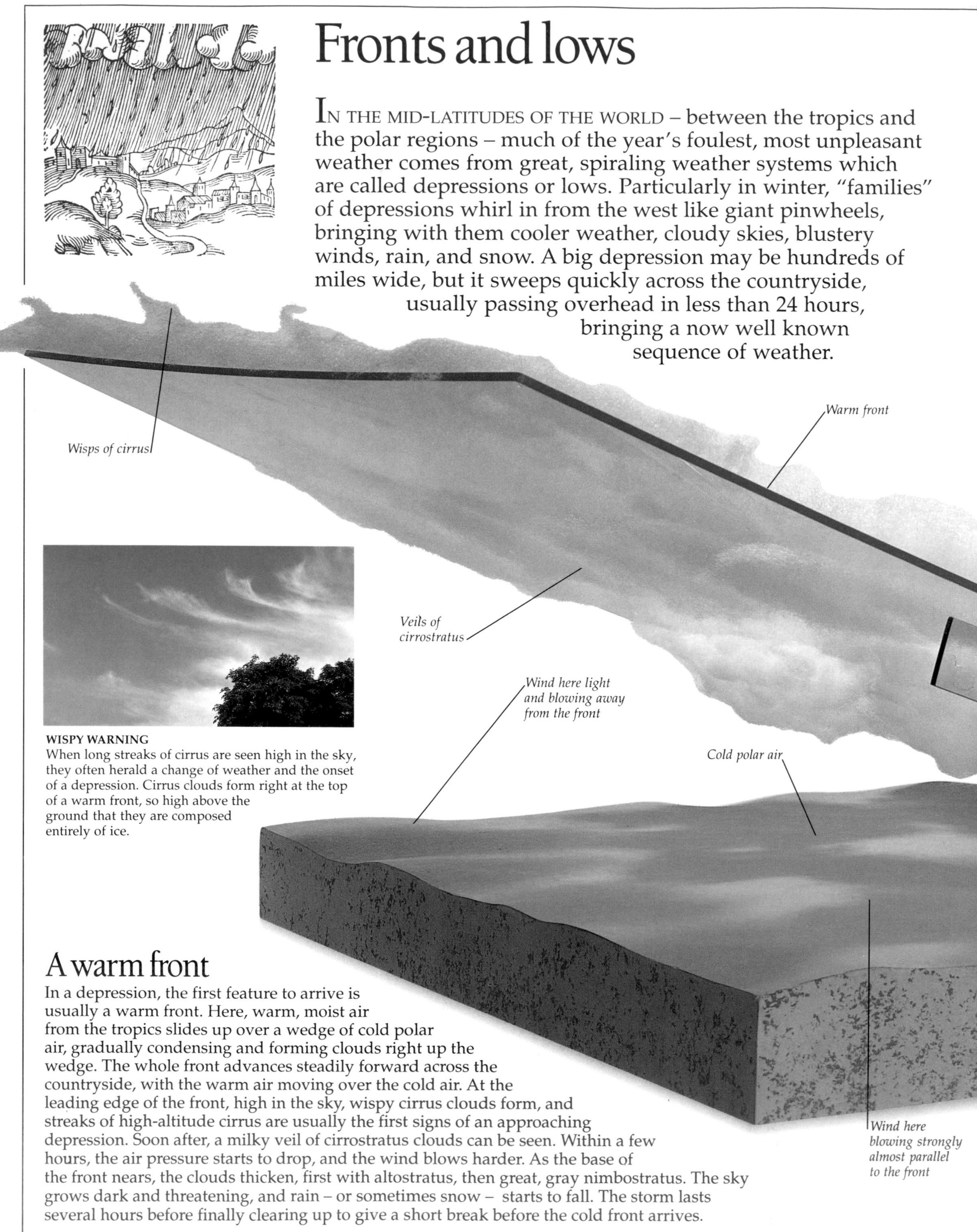

WISPY WARNING
When long streaks of cirrus are seen high in the sky, they often herald a change of weather and the onset of a depression. Cirrus clouds form right at the top of a warm front, so high above the ground that they are composed entirely of ice.

A warm front

In a depression, the first feature to arrive is usually a warm front. Here, warm, moist air from the tropics slides up over a wedge of cold polar air, gradually condensing and forming clouds right up the wedge. The whole front advances steadily forward across the countryside, with the warm air moving over the cold air. At the leading edge of the front, high in the sky, wispy cirrus clouds form, and streaks of high-altitude cirrus are usually the first signs of an approaching depression. Soon after, a milky veil of cirrostratus clouds can be seen. Within a few hours, the air pressure starts to drop, and the wind blows harder. As the base of the front nears, the clouds thicken, first with altostratus, then great, gray nimbostratus. The sky grows dark and threatening, and rain – or sometimes snow – starts to fall. The storm lasts several hours before finally clearing up to give a short break before the cold front arrives.

Masses of air

There is a close link between the direction of the wind and the weather. In the mid-latitudes, for instance, westerly winds generally bring rain and storms. Wind and weather are linked by air masses, which are vast chunks of the atmosphere almost uniformly wet or dry, cold or warm throughout. Dry, cold air masses form over continents near the poles, for instance, while warm, moist masses form over tropical oceans. All the world can be divided into areas dominated by particular air masses, each giving its own kind of weather, whether it is biting cold or warm and wet. To a large extent the weather depends on which air mass is overhead at the time. Far inland, a single air mass can stay in place for long periods at a time, bringing stable weather. In coastal areas, a shift in wind direction often brings in the influence of a different air mass and a change in the weather. The stormiest, most changeable weather tends to occur along fronts, where two air masses meet.

TO EACH ITS OWN
Each part of the world has its own particular air mass. The nature of each air mass, and the kind of weather it brings, depends on whether it forms over land or sea, near the cold poles or in the warm tropics. Warm, wet, tropical ocean air brings warm, humid weather; cold, wet, polar ocean air can bring snow. North America's East Coast, near the meeting point of several air masses, experiences changeable weather.

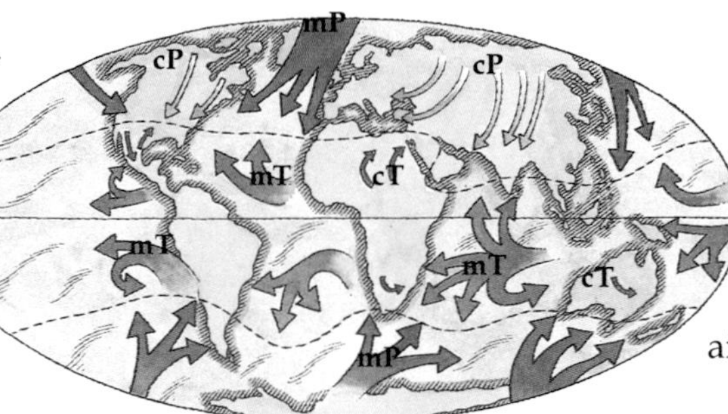

Tropical continental (cT) Polar continental (cP)
Tropical maritime (mT) Polar maritime (mP)

VEILED WARNING
When the sun is faintly visible through a thin veil of altostratus, it is time to begin seeking shelter, for rain is not far away.

FIRST RAIN
As the front approaches, the sky darkens and the first drops of rain may begin to fall – even before the thickest nimbostratus clouds arrive.

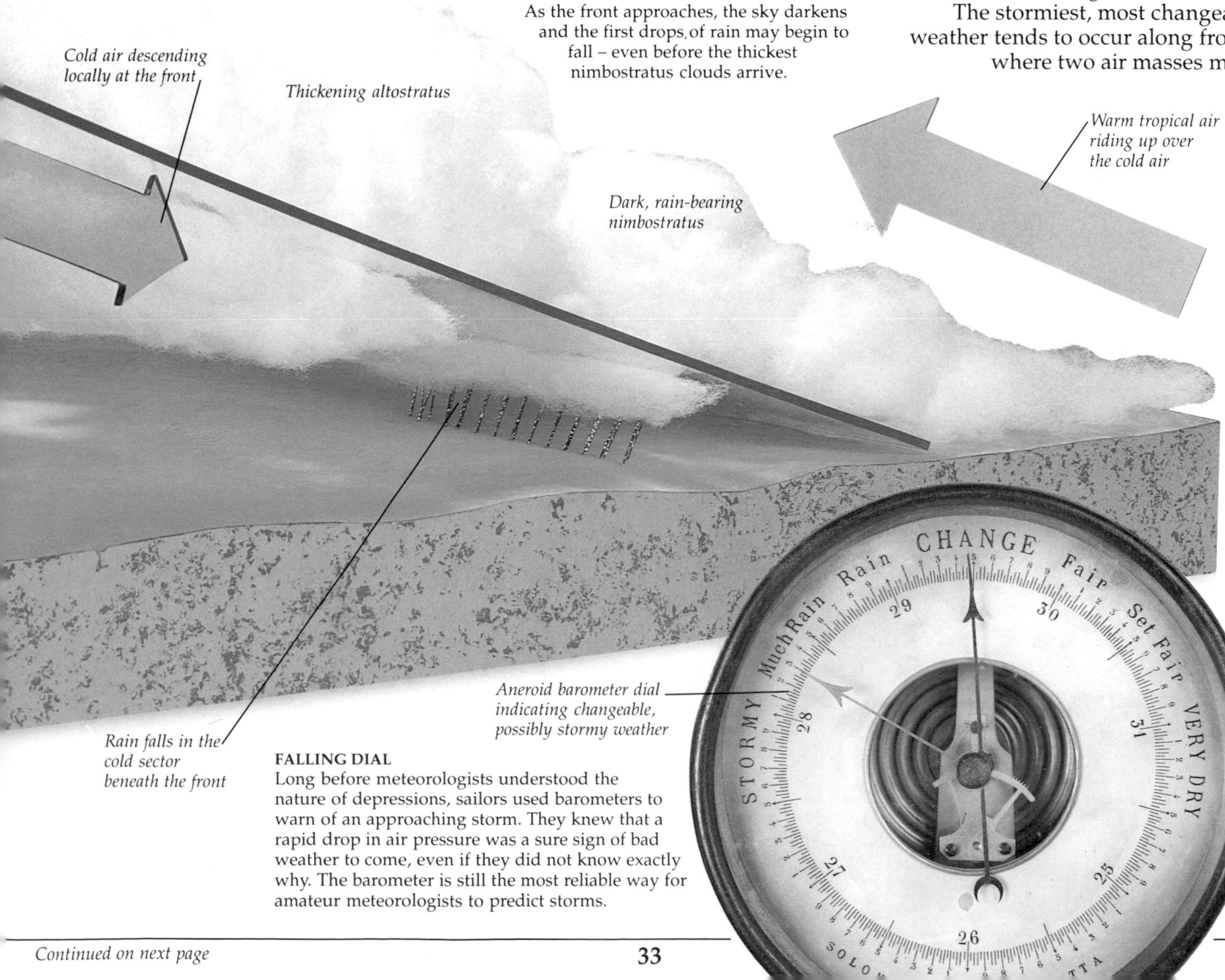

Cold air descending locally at the front

Thickening altostratus

Warm tropical air riding up over the cold air

Dark, rain-bearing nimbostratus

Rain falls in the cold sector beneath the front

Aneroid barometer dial indicating changeable, possibly stormy weather

FALLING DIAL
Long before meteorologists understood the nature of depressions, sailors used barometers to warn of an approaching storm. They knew that a rapid drop in air pressure was a sure sign of bad weather to come, even if they did not know exactly why. The barometer is still the most reliable way for amateur meteorologists to predict storms.

Continued on next page

A cold front

After the warm front has passed, the weather becomes milder, and the air pressure drops more slowly. The sky brightens a little as thick nimbostratus give way to stratocumulus. Before long, the clouds may clear away altogether. But the lull is short-lived. Thickening cumulus clouds warn of the coming cold front, where cold polar air cuts in sharply beneath the warm, moist tropical air. The cold front slopes much more steeply than the warm front, and strong updrafts can stir up violent storms. Huge cumulonimbus may build up all along the front, bringing heavy rain and sometimes thunderstorms as it passes over. But though the storms can be intense, the worst is usually over within an hour or so. As the front moves away, the air becomes colder and soon the clouds blow away, leaving just a few fair-weather cumulus scudding across the sky.

STORM WARNING
For many years, sailors were warned of coming storms by a coded system of cones, or "cautionary signals," hoisted at coastguard stations.

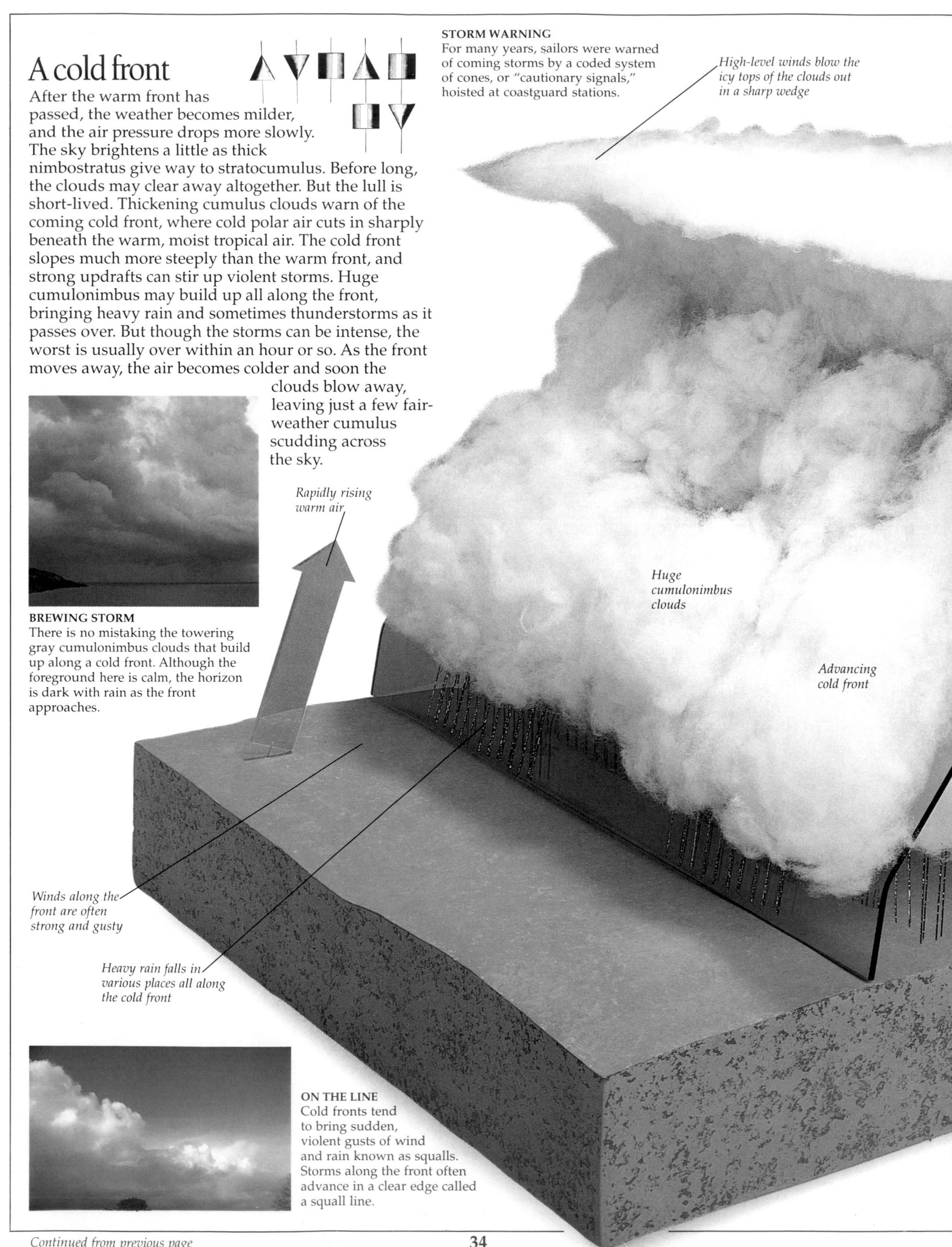

BREWING STORM
There is no mistaking the towering gray cumulonimbus clouds that build up along a cold front. Although the foreground here is calm, the horizon is dark with rain as the front approaches.

ON THE LINE
Cold fronts tend to bring sudden, violent gusts of wind and rain known as squalls. Storms along the front often advance in a clear edge called a squall line.

Continued from previous page

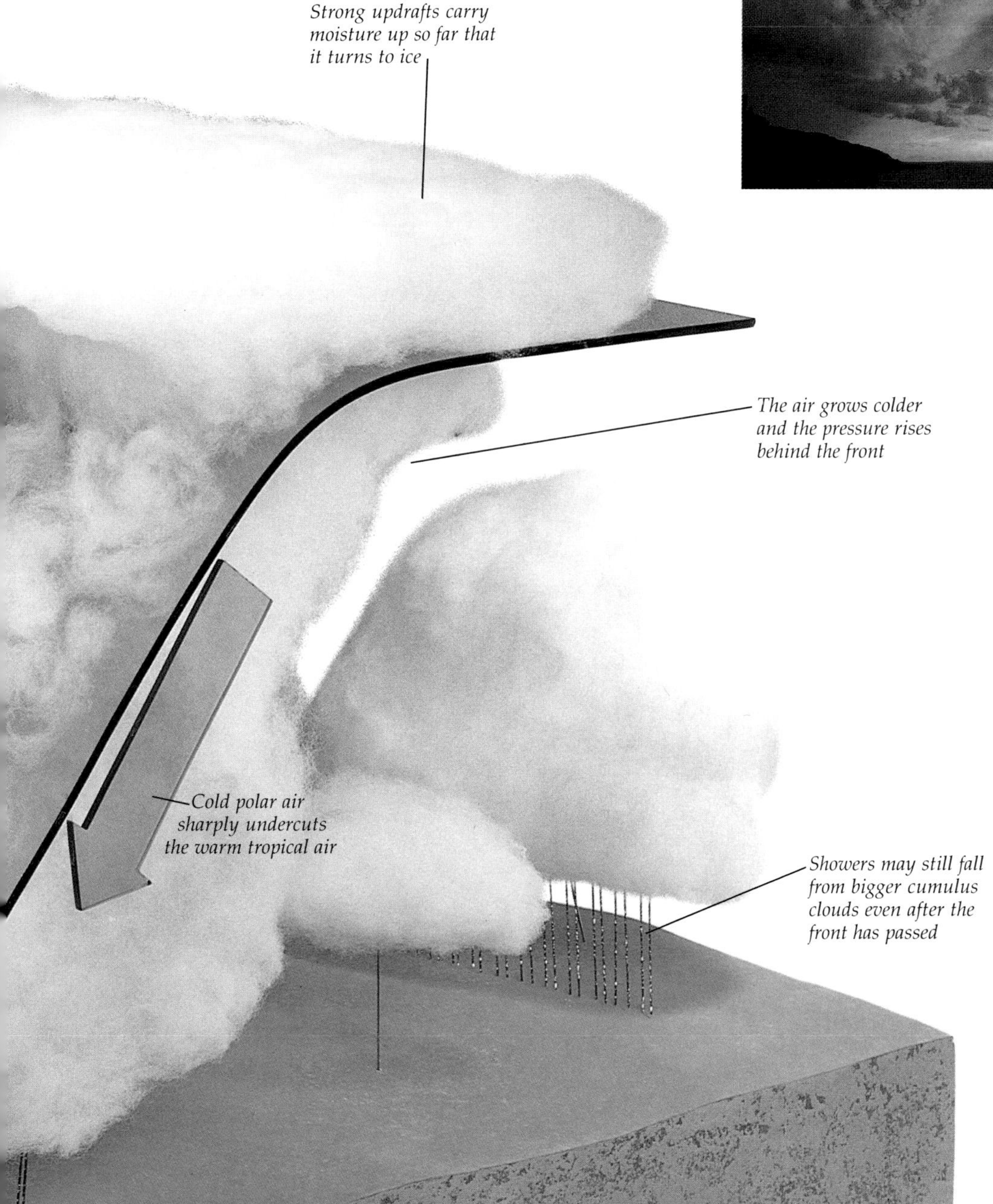

Strong updrafts carry moisture up so far that it turns to ice

The air grows colder and the pressure rises behind the front

Cold polar air sharply undercuts the warm tropical air

Showers may still fall from bigger cumulus clouds even after the front has passed

SUNSET CALM
As the front moves away to the east, the skies clear, leaving just a few puffy cumulus clouds toward the setting sun. High above, the strong upper atmosphere winds driving the depression create dramatic streaks of icy clouds across the sky.

These diagrams show the sequence in the northern hemisphere; for the south, hold a mirror above each picture.

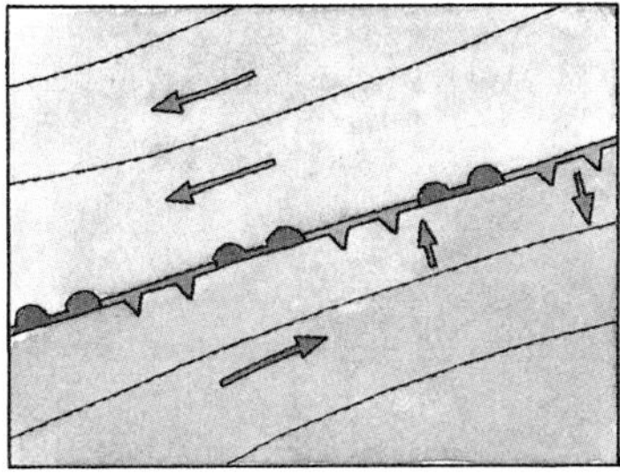

1. Depressions start with a bulge in the polar front, where cold polar air and warm tropical air meet.

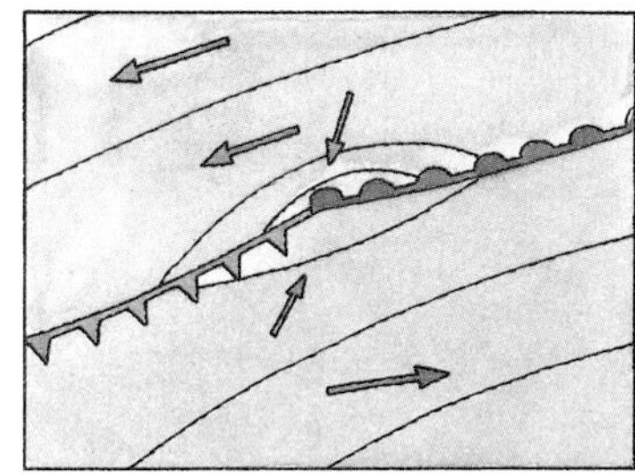

2. Spun by the Coriolis Effect (pp. 42–43), the two air masses rotate round a deepening low pressure area.

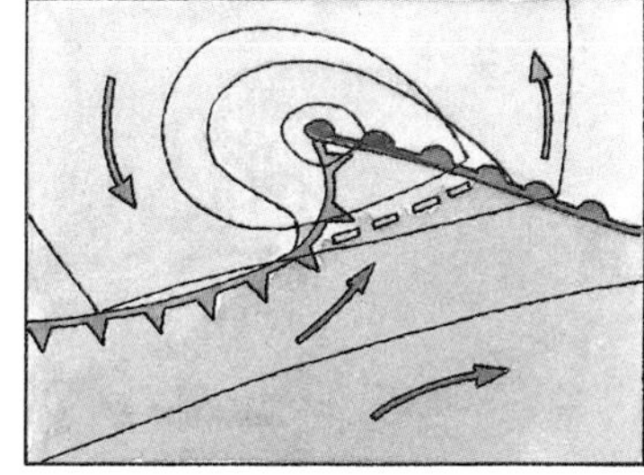

3. The kink in the front develops two arms – the warm front and the cold front – and moves slowly eastward.

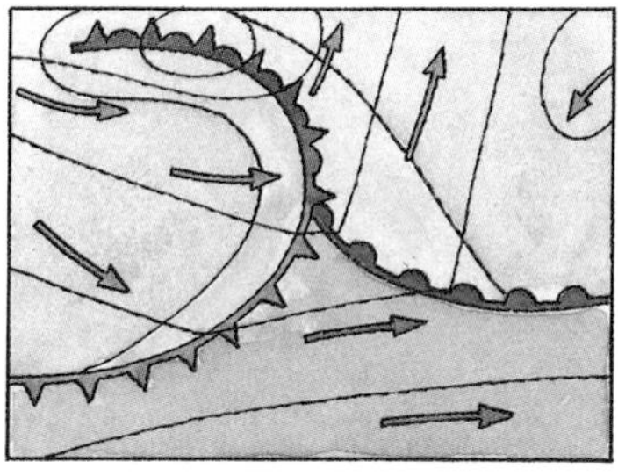

4. Eventually the cold front catches up with the warm front, lifting it off the ground to create an "occluded" front.

The life of a depression

Many depressions begin their lives over the sea. Here, warm, moist, tropical air masses and cold, dry, polar air masses collide along an imaginary line called "the polar front." A depression starts when the tropical air bulges poleward into the polar air. As the warm tropical air rises over the cold polar air, it creates an area of low pressure at the crest of the bulge. The polar air rushes in behind to replace the rising warm air. Soon winds begin to spiral around the low pressure center as cold chases warm. The depression deepens, and the polar front starts to develop a definite kink. Along one edge, the warm air continues to ride slowly forward over the cold air in a gradual slope (the warm front). Along the other, the cold air thrusts sharply under the warm air from behind (the cold front). The depression deepens further and is drawn slowly eastward by strong winds in the upper atmosphere.

Thunder and lightning

When a black, lowering cumulonimbus cloud unleashes its deluge of thunder, lightning, wind, and rain, the effect can be truly awe-inspiring. Big thunderclouds tower 10 miles (16 km) or more in the air – occasionally through the tropopause and into the stratosphere (pp. 6–7) – and churn within them enough energy to light a small town for a year. Building up a cloud of such phenomenal depth and power demands tremendously vigorous updrafts – the kind that often occur along cold fronts or above areas of ground heated especially strongly by hot sunshine. This is why, in the tropics, massive thunderstorms often break in the afternoon, after a morning's sun has stirred up the air. Inland, in the temperate zone, a long spell of hot weather often ends in a tumult of thunder and lightning.

THUNDERSTRUCK
The heavy hammer wielded by Thor, the Norse god of thunder, represented the "thunderbolt" once thought to fall from the clouds.

IT'S ELECTRIC!
In 1752, Benjamin Franklin had a lucky escape from death when proving that lightning was electricity. He flew a silk kite in a thunderstorm and saw sparks jumping from a key on the string to his hand.

LIGHTNING GENERATOR
Thunderclouds are heaving masses of air, water, and ice. Inside, ice crystals are swept up and down by the violent air currents and grow into hailstones, as water freezes around them in layers like the skins of an onion. Ice crystals and water droplets are torn apart and then smashed together with such ferocity that they become charged with static electricity. Light, positively charged pieces of ice and water tend to pile up toward the top of the cloud, and heavier, negatively charged pieces accumulate at the base. The ground below is also positively charged. The difference in electrical charges eventually becomes so great that they are neutralized by lightning flashing within the cloud (sheet lightning), or between the cloud and the ground (fork lightning).

STORM GOD
To ward off violent storms and tropical downpours, Yoruba priests in south-western Nigeria held ceremonies around images of the thunder-and-lightning god Sango.

STRIKE!
Lightning tends to strike tall objects, such as isolated trees – which is why it is dangerous to take shelter under one in a storm.

HAVING A BALL
Throughout history, many people have reported seeing a strange phenomenon called ball lightning. In 1773, just after a clap of thunder, two clergy-men saw a tiny, bright ball, no bigger than a football, glow in the fireplace, then burst with a bang. No one can explain these rare sightings.

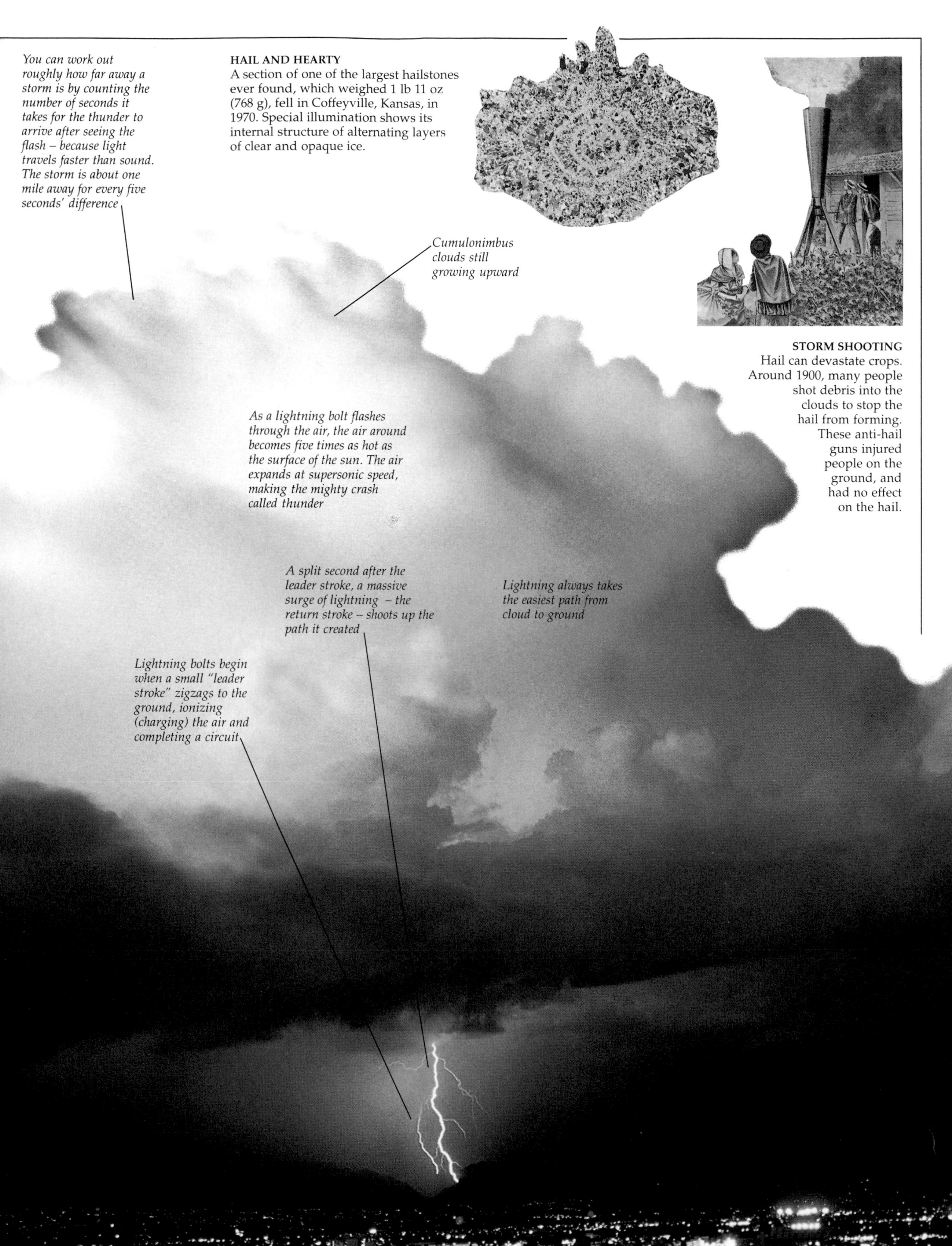

HAIL AND HEARTY
A section of one of the largest hailstones ever found, which weighed 1 lb 11 oz (768 g), fell in Coffeyville, Kansas, in 1970. Special illumination shows its internal structure of alternating layers of clear and opaque ice.

STORM SHOOTING
Hail can devastate crops. Around 1900, many people shot debris into the clouds to stop the hail from forming. These anti-hail guns injured people on the ground, and had no effect on the hail.

TROPICAL STORM
The monsoon can lash tropical coasts with intense rain, wind, thunder, and lightning.

Monsoon

For six months of the year, most of India is parched and dry. But, every May, the monsoon comes. A moist wind starts to blow in from the Indian Ocean, and the skies over the southwest coast grow dark with clouds. For six months, showers of torrential rain sweep north over the country, right up to the foothills of the Himalayas – until, in October, the southwest wind dies down and the rains slacken. By the end of the year, the land is dry once more. The monsoon is especially marked in India, but similar rainy seasons occur in many other places in the tropics, including northeast Australia, East Africa, and the southern United States.

The monsoon brings some of the world's most torrential rains

Band of rain moving rapidly across open grassland

DRAGON'S BREATH
The monsoon rains are vital for agriculture in most of Asia. To the Chinese their importance was symbolized by the dragon, a creature of the heavens and of the rivers – at times violent, but also the bearer of the precious gift of water.

AFTER THE DELUGE
Monsoon rain can be so intense that floods are frequent. In India and Bangladesh, the delta of the Ganges River is in particular danger of being flooded, especially if a storm surge occurs at the same time (pp. 44–45).

Wind-disk for tracking the path of the typhoon

Heavy needle lines up with the normal path of storms in the region

Thin needle indicates safe course away from the storm

Typhoon barometer

Arrows on the disk for the direction of the wind over the ship. The disk is turned until an arrow crosses the heavy needle in the right direction

TYPHOON TRACKER
Ships at sea around many monsoon regions often fall foul of ferocious, fast-moving tropical cyclones, or typhoons. To help track the path of the storm and steer a safe course, many ships used to carry an instrument like this, called a baryocyclometer. Now most rely on broadcast warnings.

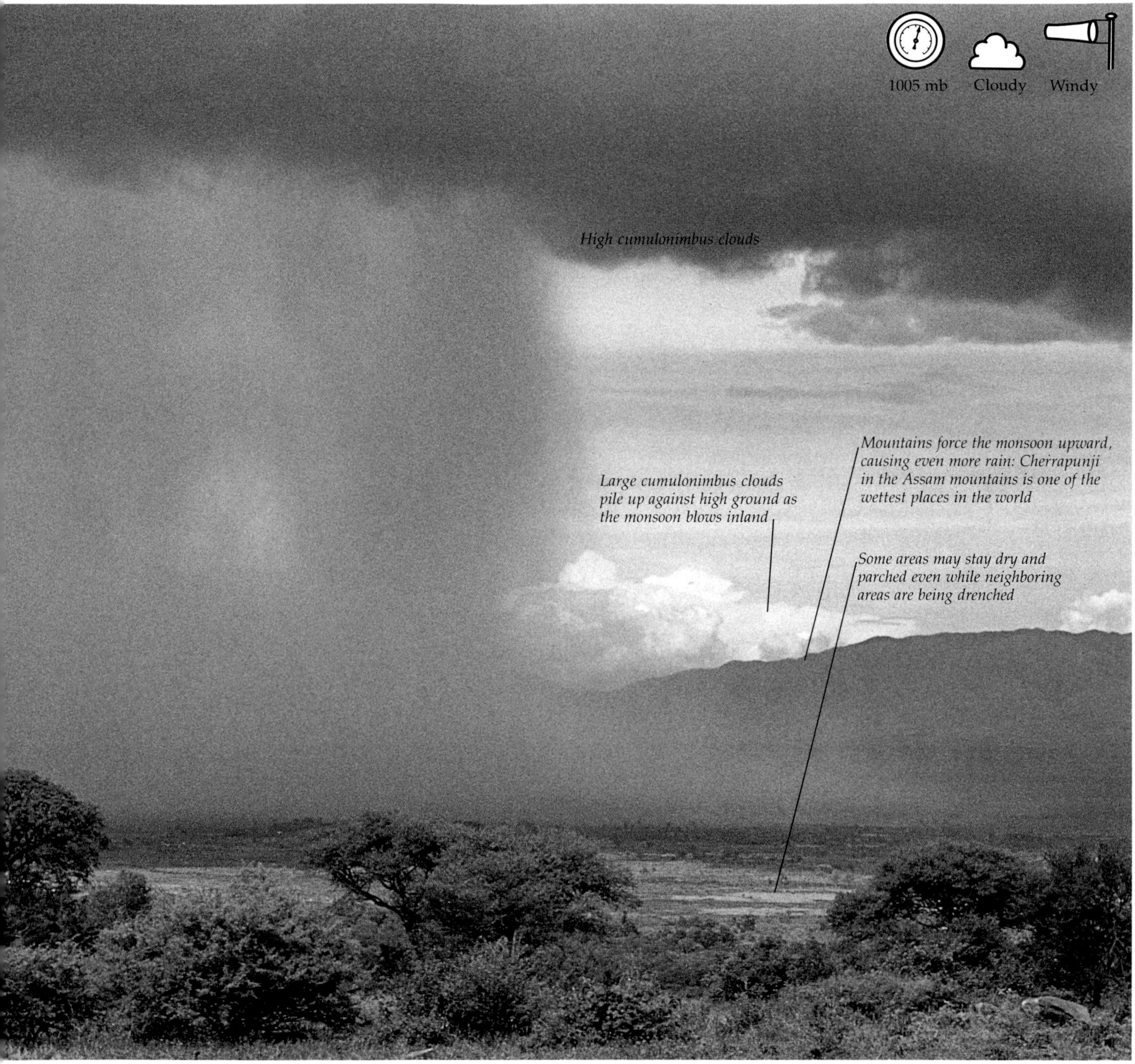

1005 mb
Cloudy
Windy
High cumulonimbus clouds
Mountains force the monsoon upward, causing even more rain: Cherrapunji in the Assam mountains is one of the wettest places in the world
Large cumulonimbus clouds pile up against high ground as the monsoon blows inland
Some areas may stay dry and parched even while neighboring areas are being drenched

THE MONSOON COMES
Monsoons are like giant sea breezes (pp. 56–57). The rains begin when summer sun heats up tropical land masses far faster than the surrounding oceans. Warm air rising over land draws in cool, moist air from the sea, and rain-bearing winds gradually push farther inland. A monsoon's onset is hard to predict, and sometimes it fails to bring any rain to the hot, drought-stricken lands that year. Then crops fail, with a great danger of famine. Asian monsoons may be triggered when westerly jet streams in the upper air swing north over the Himalayas.

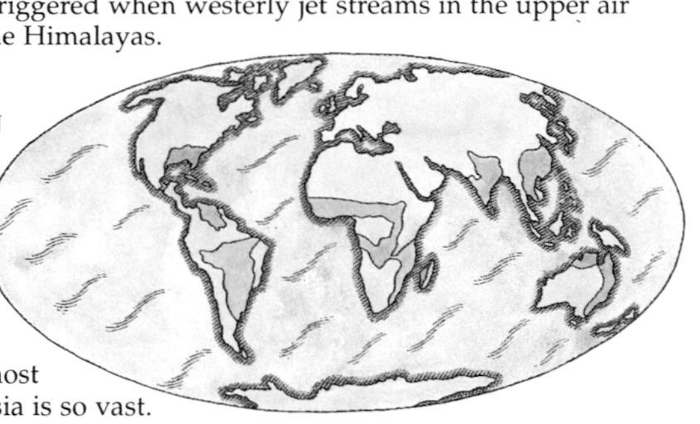

MONSOON REGION
Monsoons affect large areas of the tropics and the sub-tropics from northeast Australia to the Caribbean. Asian monsoons are the most extreme, because Asia is so vast.

Himalayas
Rain clouds
Warm sea
Cold land
Moist southwest monsoon bringing rain
Indian Ocean

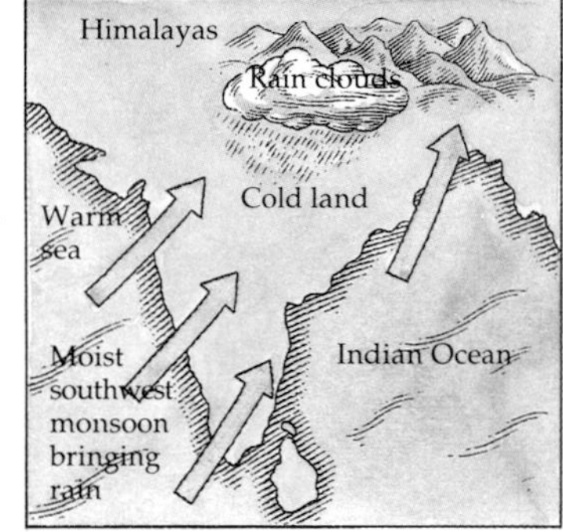

SOUTHWEST MONSOON
The hot, dry lands of Asia draw warm air, laden with moisture, in from the Indian Ocean during the early summer.

Hot land
Dry northeast monsoon
Cool sea

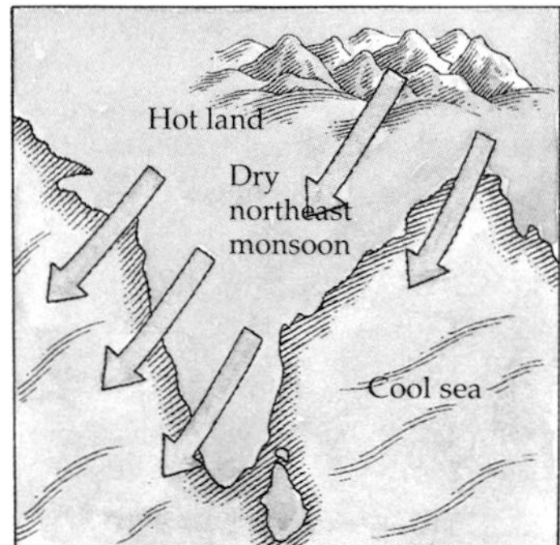

NORTHEAST MONSOON
The cold, dry winter air spreads out from central Asia, bringing chilly, dusty conditions to the lands around.

A snowy day

ST. BERNARDS TO THE RESCUE
Freshly fallen snow contains so much air that people can survive for a long time beneath it.

IN THE DEPTHS OF WINTER, driving snow and blizzards may fall from the same gray clouds and fronts that in summer brought welcome showers. Outside the tropics, most rain starts off as snow, melting as it drops into warmer air. When snow falls, the air is just cold enough to let the flakes flutter to the ground before they melt. Sometimes, snow can be falling on the mountaintop while down in the valley it is raining. People often say the weather is "too cold for snow," and there is some truth in this, since very cold air may not hold enough moisture for any kind of precipitation (pp. 22–23). In fact, more snow falls in a year in southern Canada and the northern USA than at the North Pole. The heaviest snowfalls occur when the air temperature is hovering around freezing – which is why snow can be hard to forecast, because a rise in temperature of just a few degrees above freezing may bring rain instead.

Under very cold conditions snow remains loose and powdery, and is often whipped up by the wind

Fresh snow can contain as much as 90–95 percent air and acts as an insulator, protecting the ground from much colder temperatures above the surface

A COLD BLANKET
Once snow has covered the ground, it is often slow to melt, because it reflects most of the sunlight. If the surface melts partially and then refreezes, the snow cover will last even longer. Only the arrival of a warm air mass is really effective in melting the snow.

RIVERS OF ICE AND AIR
Snow accumulates on high ground where temperatures are low. It becomes compacted, or squeezed, into ice, which slowly flows down valleys as glaciers. The air above large icecaps becomes very cold and heavy, and follows the same paths, bringing icy winds to the lowlands beneath.

SNOWFLAKES
Snowflakes occur in an infinite variety of shapes, and no one has ever found two the same. All natural snowflakes are six-sided and consist of ice crystals which are flat plates; rarer forms like needles and columns are sometimes found.

THE SNOWFLAKE MAN
W. A. Bentley was an American farmer who spent every possible moment out in the cold, photographing snowflakes through a microscope. Over the course of 40 years he made thousands of photographs.

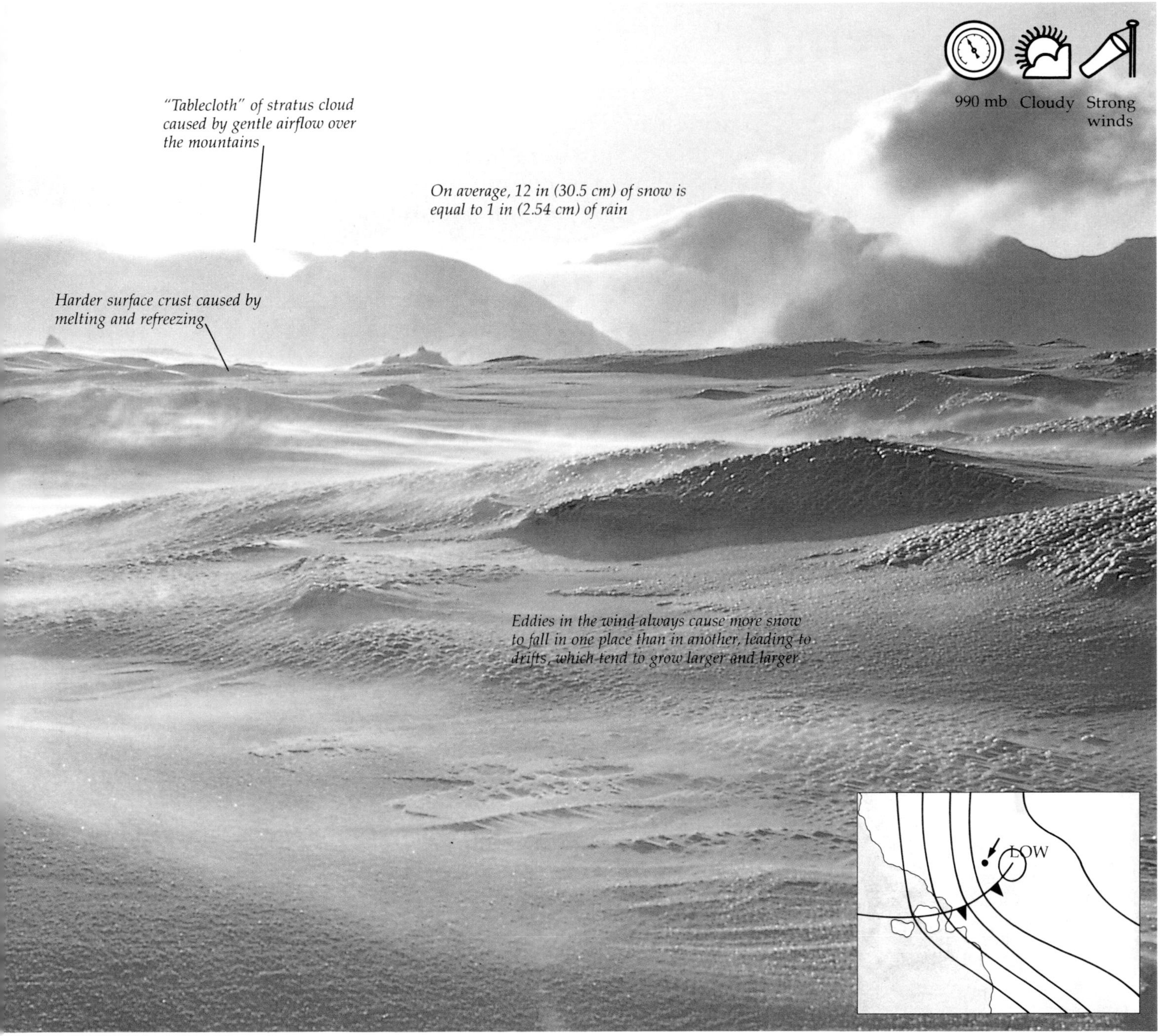

990 mb Cloudy Strong winds

"Tablecloth" of stratus cloud caused by gentle airflow over the mountains

On average, 12 in (30.5 cm) of snow is equal to 1 in (2.54 cm) of rain

Harder surface crust caused by melting and refreezing

Eddies in the wind always cause more snow to fall in one place than in another, leading to drifts, which tend to grow larger and larger

LOW

AVALANCHE
The greatest danger of avalanches comes when fresh, loose snow has fallen onto a harder, icy layer. The slightest disturbance can start a slide, which crashes down into the valley, burying anything and anyone in its path. The blast of air in front of it is often strong enough to demolish buildings.

BLIZZARD
In blizzard conditions, snowfall is accompanied by strong winds, and it may become impossible to see anything, causing problems in travel and communications in both cities and the countryside. The wind piles huge drifts of snow against any obstacle and may completely cover cars and trains, trapping the passengers inside.

Wind

THE WORLD'S ATMOSPHERE is forever on the move. Wind is air in motion. Sometimes air moves slowly, giving a gentle breeze. At other times it moves rapidly, creating gales and hurricanes (pp. 44–45). Gentle or fierce, wind always starts in the same way. As the sun moves through the sky, it heats up some parts of the sea and land more than others. The air above these hot spots is warmed, becomes lighter than the surrounding air, and begins to rise. Elsewhere, cool air sinks, because it is heavier. Winds blow because air squeezed out by sinking, cold air is sucked in under rising, warm air. Winds will blow wherever there is a difference in air temperature and pressure, always flowing from high to low pressure. Some winds blow in one place, and have a local name – North America's chinook and France's mistral. Others are part of a huge circulation pattern that sends winds over the entire globe.

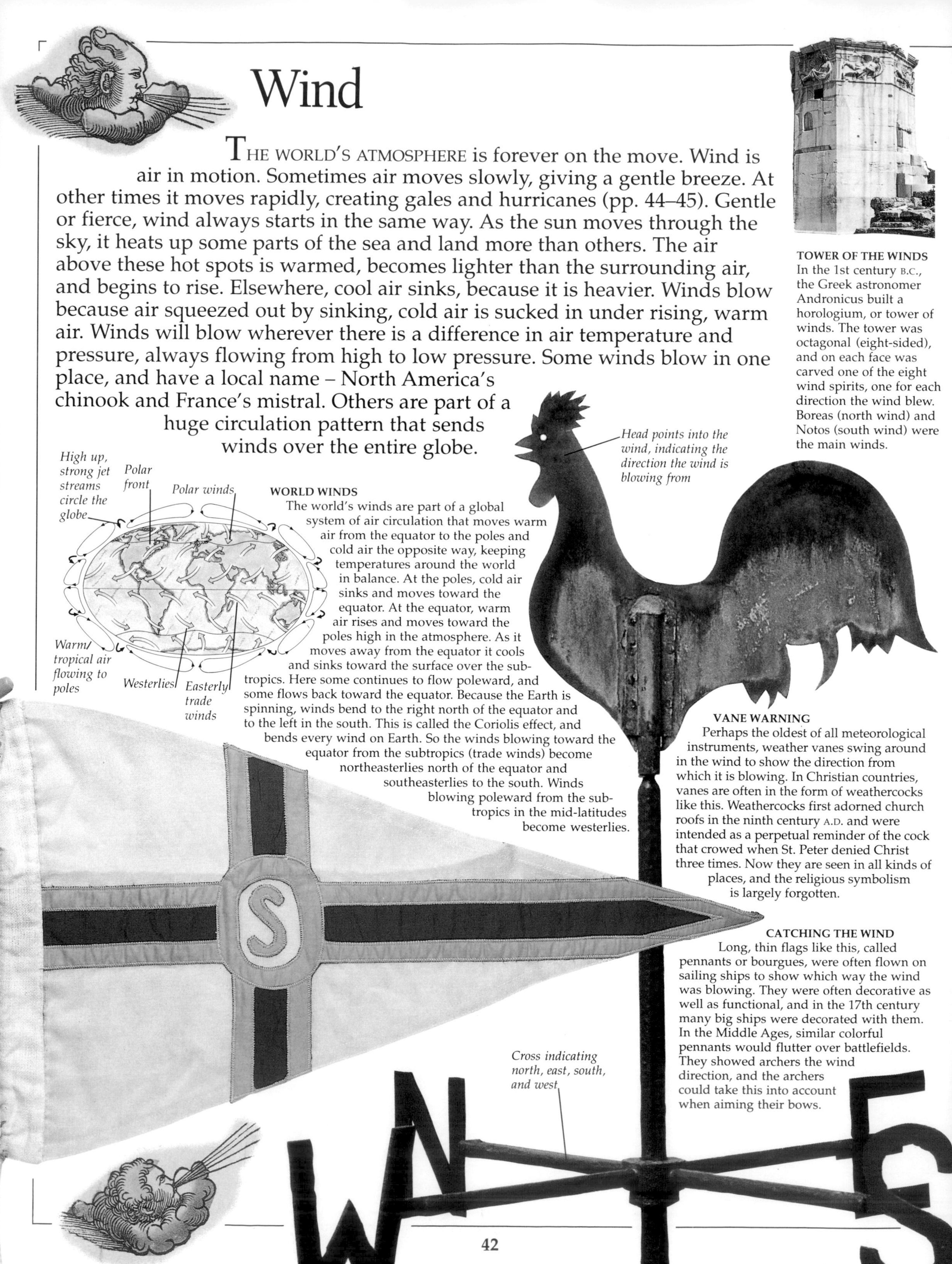

TOWER OF THE WINDS
In the 1st century B.C., the Greek astronomer Andronicus built a horologium, or tower of winds. The tower was octagonal (eight-sided), and on each face was carved one of the eight wind spirits, one for each direction the wind blew. Boreas (north wind) and Notos (south wind) were the main winds.

WORLD WINDS
The world's winds are part of a global system of air circulation that moves warm air from the equator to the poles and cold air the opposite way, keeping temperatures around the world in balance. At the poles, cold air sinks and moves toward the equator. At the equator, warm air rises and moves toward the poles high in the atmosphere. As it moves away from the equator it cools and sinks toward the surface over the subtropics. Here some continues to flow poleward, and some flows back toward the equator. Because the Earth is spinning, winds bend to the right north of the equator and to the left in the south. This is called the Coriolis effect, and bends every wind on Earth. So the winds blowing toward the equator from the subtropics (trade winds) become northeasterlies north of the equator and southeasterlies to the south. Winds blowing poleward from the subtropics in the mid-latitudes become westerlies.

VANE WARNING
Perhaps the oldest of all meteorological instruments, weather vanes swing around in the wind to show the direction from which it is blowing. In Christian countries, vanes are often in the form of weathercocks like this. Weathercocks first adorned church roofs in the ninth century A.D. and were intended as a perpetual reminder of the cock that crowed when St. Peter denied Christ three times. Now they are seen in all kinds of places, and the religious symbolism is largely forgotten.

CATCHING THE WIND
Long, thin flags like this, called pennants or bourgues, were often flown on sailing ships to show which way the wind was blowing. They were often decorative as well as functional, and in the 17th century many big ships were decorated with them. In the Middle Ages, similar colorful pennants would flutter over battlefields. They showed archers the wind direction, and the archers could take this into account when aiming their bows.

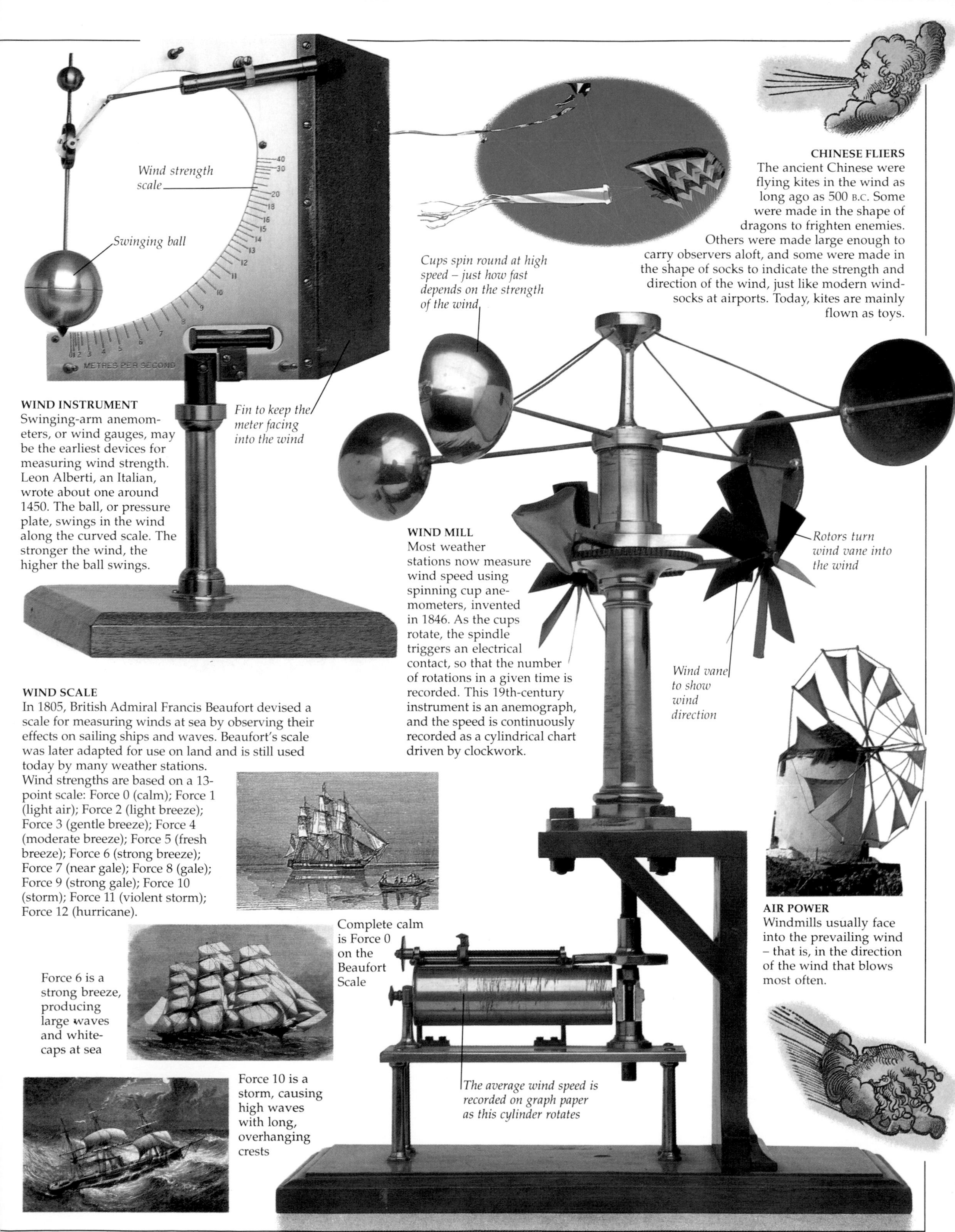

CHINESE FLIERS
The ancient Chinese were flying kites in the wind as long ago as 500 B.C. Some were made in the shape of dragons to frighten enemies. Others were made large enough to carry observers aloft, and some were made in the shape of socks to indicate the strength and direction of the wind, just like modern windsocks at airports. Today, kites are mainly flown as toys.

WIND INSTRUMENT
Swinging-arm anemometers, or wind gauges, may be the earliest devices for measuring wind strength. Leon Alberti, an Italian, wrote about one around 1450. The ball, or pressure plate, swings in the wind along the curved scale. The stronger the wind, the higher the ball swings.

WIND MILL
Most weather stations now measure wind speed using spinning cup anemometers, invented in 1846. As the cups rotate, the spindle triggers an electrical contact, so that the number of rotations in a given time is recorded. This 19th-century instrument is an anemograph, and the speed is continuously recorded as a cylindrical chart driven by clockwork.

WIND SCALE
In 1805, British Admiral Francis Beaufort devised a scale for measuring winds at sea by observing their effects on sailing ships and waves. Beaufort's scale was later adapted for use on land and is still used today by many weather stations. Wind strengths are based on a 13-point scale: Force 0 (calm); Force 1 (light air); Force 2 (light breeze); Force 3 (gentle breeze); Force 4 (moderate breeze); Force 5 (fresh breeze); Force 6 (strong breeze); Force 7 (near gale); Force 8 (gale); Force 9 (strong gale); Force 10 (storm); Force 11 (violent storm); Force 12 (hurricane).

Complete calm is Force 0 on the Beaufort Scale

Force 6 is a strong breeze, producing large waves and whitecaps at sea

Force 10 is a storm, causing high waves with long, overhanging crests

AIR POWER
Windmills usually face into the prevailing wind – that is, in the direction of the wind that blows most often.

Tropical storms

Hurricane force winds often damage buildings

KNOWN AS TYPHOONS IN THE PACIFIC, and tropical cyclones by meteorologists, hurricanes claim more lives each year than any other storms. When a full-blown hurricane strikes, trees are ripped up and buildings flattened by raging winds, gusting up to 220 mph (360 km/h). Vast areas are swamped by torrential rain, and coastal regions can be completely overwhelmed by the "storm surge," This is a mound of water some 25 ft (8 m) high, sucked up by the storm's "eye" – the ring of low pressure at the storm's centre – and topped by giant waves whipped up by the winds. Hurricanes begin as small thunderstorms over warm, tropical oceans. If the water is warm enough (over 80°F/27°C), several storms may cluster together and whirl around as one, encouraged by strong winds high in the atmosphere. Soon, they drift westward across the ocean, drawing in warm, moist air and spinning in ever tighter circles. At first, the center of the storm may be over 200 miles (300 km) across, and the winds barely gale force. As it moves west, it gains energy from the warm air it sucks in. By the time the storm reaches the far side of the ocean, the eye has shrunk to 30 miles (50 km) across, pressure there has dropped dramatically, and winds howl around it at hurricane force.

ANATOMY OF A HURRICANE
The air in the eye of the hurricane is at low pressure, and is calm. As the eye passes over, the winds may drop altogether, and a small circle of clear sky may be visible overhead for a while. The lull is short-lived, however, as torrential rains fall around the eye, and raging winds, drawn in from hot air that spirals up the wall of the eye, circulate at speeds of at least 75 mph (120 km/h). The rain and wind are at their worst right next to the eye of the storm, but spiraling bands of rain and wind can occur up to 240 miles (400 km) away. It can be 18 hours or more before the storm has passed over completely.

MIXED BLESSING
The vegetation and agriculture on many tropical islands depend on the torrential rains brought by hurricanes. But the terrible winds can also ravage crops, and only a few – like bananas – recover quickly.

The strongest winds, with gusts up to 225 mph (360 kph) are found beneath the eye wall, immediately outside the eye

HURRICANE WATCH
Thanks to satellite images, meteorologists can detect hurricanes when they are far from land, and track them as they approach. Special aircraft repeatedly fly through the storm to obtain accurate measurements that help predict its violence and likely path. Since 1954, names have been given to all tropical storms and cyclones to prevent confusion when issuing forecasts and evacuation warnings.

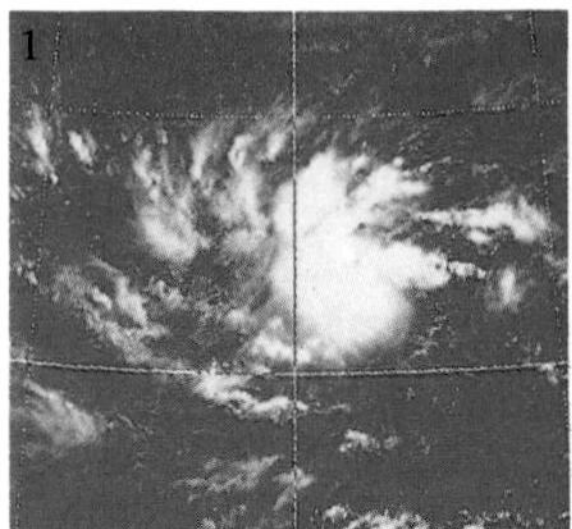

Day 1: Thunderstorms develop over the sea.

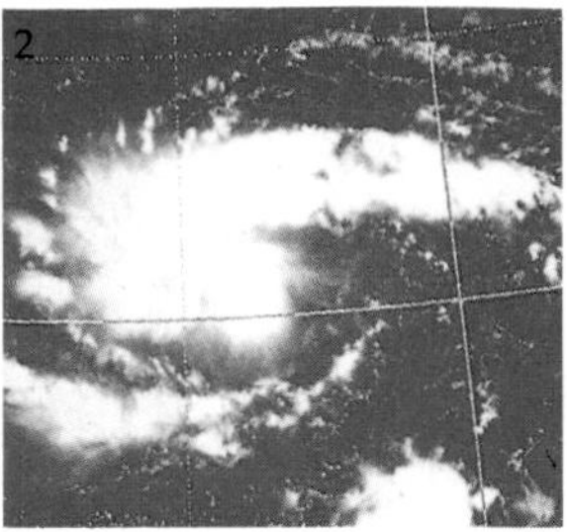

Day 2: Storms group to form a swirl of cloud.

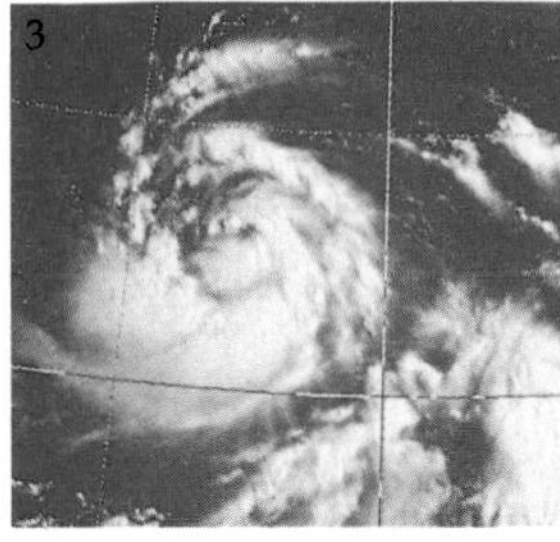

Day 4: Winds grow; distinct center forms in cloud swirl.

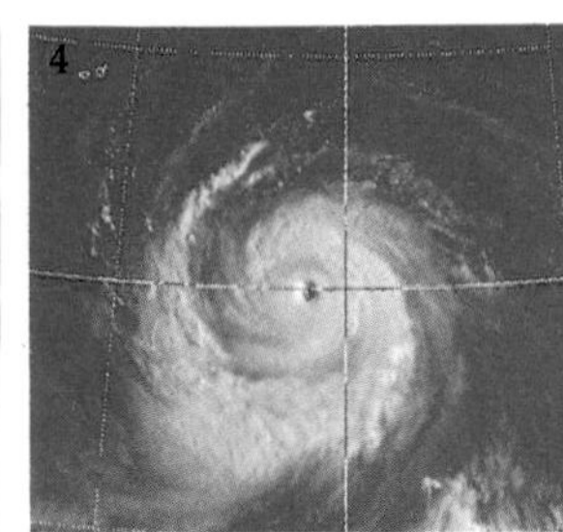

Day 7: Eye forms; typhoon is at its most dangerous.

Day 11: Eye passes over land; typhoon starts to die.

PACIFIC HURRICANE
The sequence above shows satellite images of a typhoon over the Pacific Ocean. It begins when water evaporates over vast areas of the ocean in the hot, tropical sun to produce huge cumulonimbus clouds and bands of thunderstorms (1). Gradually, a swirl of clouds develops, and the growing storm looks like a vigorous, ordinary depression (pp. 32–33) (2). The winds become even stronger, and rotate around a single center (3). Eventually an eye develops, just inside the ring of the most destructive and violent winds (4). When such a storm passes over land – in this case, Japan – or over cold seas, it loses its source of energy, and the winds drop rapidly (5).

Ice forms at the very top of the clouds

A vast circular shield of clouds is caused by air billowing from the top of the storm and spreading out

Warm, moist air spirals up around the eye inside the hurricane

Eye wall

Spiral rain bands

Hurricanes are enormous. Some may be as much as 500 miles (800 km) across

The heat contained by the warm sea provides the energy needed to drive the whole storm

Calm eye of hurricane, where winds may be no more than 15 mph (25 kph)

Air descends in the eye, leaving it clear of cloud

Winds well above 100 mph (160 kph) occur over a large area beneath the storm

ALBANY HURRICANE
Hurricanes were far more dangerous when their approach was unexpected. In 1940, the fringes of a hurricane struck Albany, Georgia, without adequate warning, wrecking large numbers of buildings, including big hotels, and killing several people. Two years before, 600 people were killed in New England by a sudden, fast-moving storm.

Whirling winds

MILD SPIN
Tornadoes are especially violent in the central USA, but they can occur anywhere there are thunderstorms, as this engraving of an English whirlwind shows.

TORNADOES GO BY MANY NAMES – twisters, whirlwinds, and more. Wherever they strike, these whirling spirals of wind leave a trail of unbelievable destruction. They roar past in just a few minutes, tossing people, cars, and buildings high into the air, then smashing them to the ground. Meteorological instruments rarely survive to tell what conditions are really like in a tornado. Winds probably race around the outside at over 240 mph (400 kph), while pressure at the center plunges several hundred millibars lower than outside. This creates a kind of funnel, or vortex, that acts like a giant vacuum cleaner, sucking things into the air, tearing the tops off trees, and blowing out windows. Tornadoes hang down like an elephant's trunk from giant thunderclouds, and may strike wherever thunderstorms occur.

1 **SWIRLING COLUMN**
Tornadoes start deep within vast thunderclouds, where a column of strongly rising warm air is set spinning by high winds streaming through the cloud's top. As air is sucked into this swirling column, or mesocyclone, it spins very fast, stretching thousands of feet up and down through the cloud, with a corkscrewing funnel descending from the cloud's base – the tornado.

CROP CIRCLES
For centuries, it has been a mystery why perfect circles of flattened crops appear at random in the summer. A few people believe that it may be whirling winds which cause them.

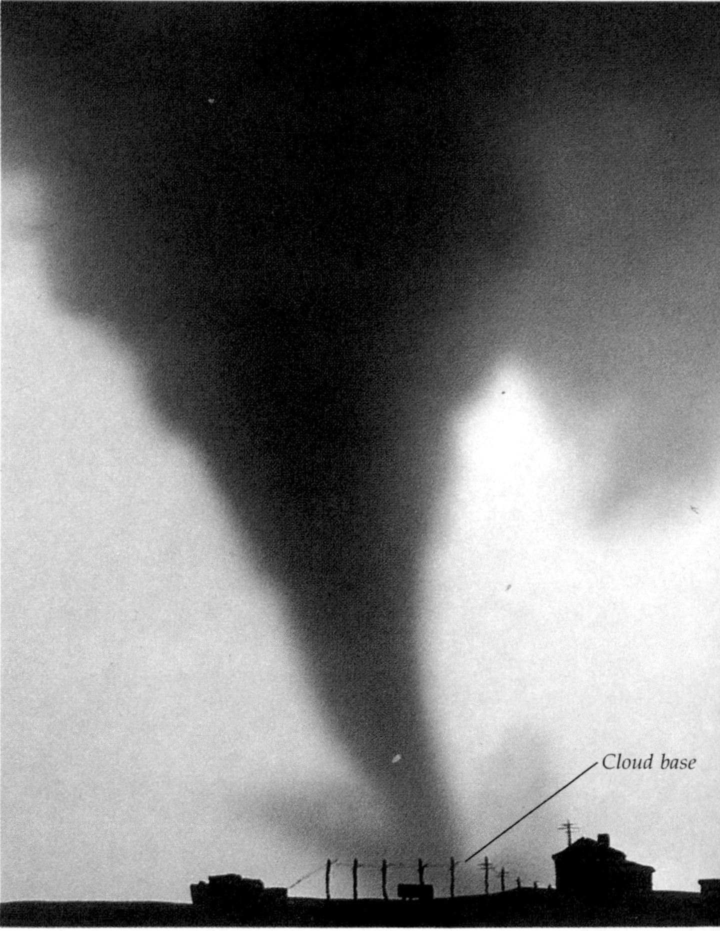

2 **WHIRLING DERVISH**
Soon the funnel touches down, and the tremendous updraft in its center swirls dust, debris, cars, and people high into the sky. Chunks of wood and other objects become deadly missiles as they are hurled through the air by the ferocious winds. A tornado deals destruction very selectively – reducing houses in its path to matchsticks and rubble, yet leaving those just a few yards outside its path completely untouched. Sometimes a tornado will whirl things high into the air, then set them gently down, unharmed, hundreds of feet away.

WATERSPOUT

When a tornado occurs over the sea, it becomes a waterspout. Waterspouts often last longer than tornadoes, but tend to be gentler, with wind speeds less than 50 mph (80 kph). This may be because water is heavier than air, and the strong temperature contrasts needed to create violent updrafts are less marked over water than land.

DUSTY MENACE

Unlike tornadoes and waterspouts, which spin down from clouds, "dust devils" are formed in the desert by columns of hot air whirling up from the ground. Although far weaker than tornadoes, they can still cause damage. Whirling devils also occur over snow and water, although these can start as violent eddies whipping up from the surface.

FLYING ROOFS *left and above*

In the strong winds of tornadoes, the roofs of houses generate lift, just like the wings of a plane. When the roof is whisked away, the rest of the house disintegrates. Stronger roofs, more firmly anchored to the buildings beneath, would prevent a great deal of damage.

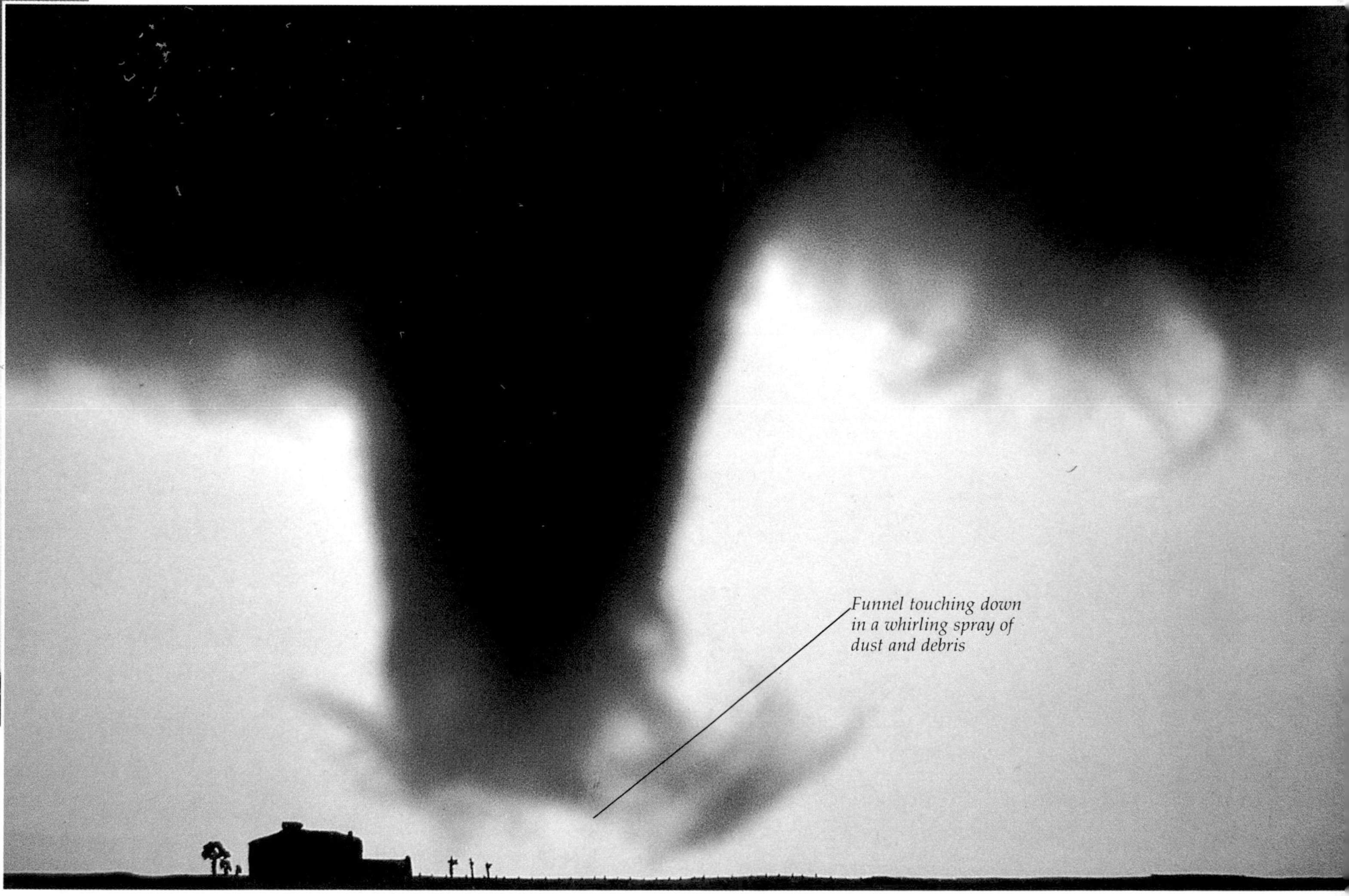

Funnel touching down in a whirling spray of dust and debris

3 SPINNING VORTEX

For a moment, the funnel has lifted away from the ground, and the houses beneath are safe. But at any instant it may touch down again. This is a large tornado, and within it there is not just one spinning vortex but several, each revolving around the rim of the main one.

Fogs and mists

BEACON IN THE DARK
Thick, persistent fog can form over such sea areas as southwestern Britain, the Banks off Newfoundland, and Tierra del Fuego at the tip of South America. In really dense fog, the lights of lighthouses, which warn ships of hazards, may be lost in the dark, and sailors must rely on sirens and foghorns.

When the wind is light, the sky is clear, and the air is damp, moisture in the air can often condense near the ground to form mist or fog, especially at dawn or dusk. In some places, dawn often breaks with thick mist hanging over the landscape like a pale, gray veil – dispersing only as the sun begins to warm the air and stir up stronger winds. Sometimes fog forms because the ground cools down enough to bring the air to its dew point (pp. 22–23), and the fog spreads slowly upward. This is called radiation fog, and often occurs on clear, fairly calm nights in areas where there is plenty of moisture, such as river valleys, lakes, and harbors. Fog can also form by "advection," where a warm, moist wind blows over a cooler surface.

Over the sea, temperature does not always fall far enough to form fog

CALIFORNIA FOG
In San Francisco, California, the distinctive towers of the Golden Gate Bridge often rise above the thick mist that rolls in from the Pacific. This fog is an advection fog, and forms because warm, moist air from the south blows over cool ocean currents flowing down from the Arctic. As it moves inland, the fog evaporates quickly over the warm surface of the land and usually thins out as it is blown in toward San Francisco. On the coast, advection fogs may take time to disperse – unlike radiation fogs – because they will break up only when there is a change in the conditions that caused them.

SMOG MASK
Urban areas are particularly prone to thick fogs, not only because they are often situated in low-lying areas close to water, but also fog forms much more readily when there are plenty of condensation nuclei (pp. 22–23) in the air. In some cities, the huge quantities of airborne particles released by car exhausts, fires, and industry make some cyclists wear masks.

PEA-SOUPER
Heavy industry and millions of coal fires once made London so dirty that the city was particularly notorious for its fogs "as thick as pea soup," when visibility would drop to 50 ft (15 m) or less. During the 1950s, government actions to clean up the air reduced the number of fogs dramatically, and such "pea-soupers" are now a thing of the past.

TWO FOGS

Some coastal fog is a mixture of both radiation and advection fog. On a clear, warm day, a sea breeze may start (pp. 56–57), bringing relatively cool, moist air across the land. At night, most of this air drifts back to sea as it is replaced by the drier land air. Some sea air may linger and cool further until it condenses to form fog.

UPSIDE DOWN

Fog forms just above the ground or water and spreads slowly upward, but only so far, because the calm, clear conditions that encourage it may cause a reversal in the normal change in temperature in the atmosphere. The air actually gets warmer around 1640 ft (500 m) above the ground. This is called a temperature inversion, and the base of the inversion marks the ceiling of the fog. Inversions like this are common in places like San Diego (right), California, and the Sydney basin in Australia.

A day of weather

THE WEATHER CAN CHANGE dramatically during the course of a single day. Sometimes these daily changes can be more striking than any long-term variations. In many tropical regions, the same marked changes in the weather occur regularly day after day, where fine, sunny mornings are almost always followed by a massive build-up of thunderclouds as the sun stirs up strong updrafts. Usually this is followed by a brief rainstorm in the afternoon and a clear dusk. A similar sequence often occurs in mid-latitudes if the weather is warm and stable. In these areas regular daily changes are often overpowered by the passage of a depression, which can swing the weather from warm sunshine to icy rain in a few hours.

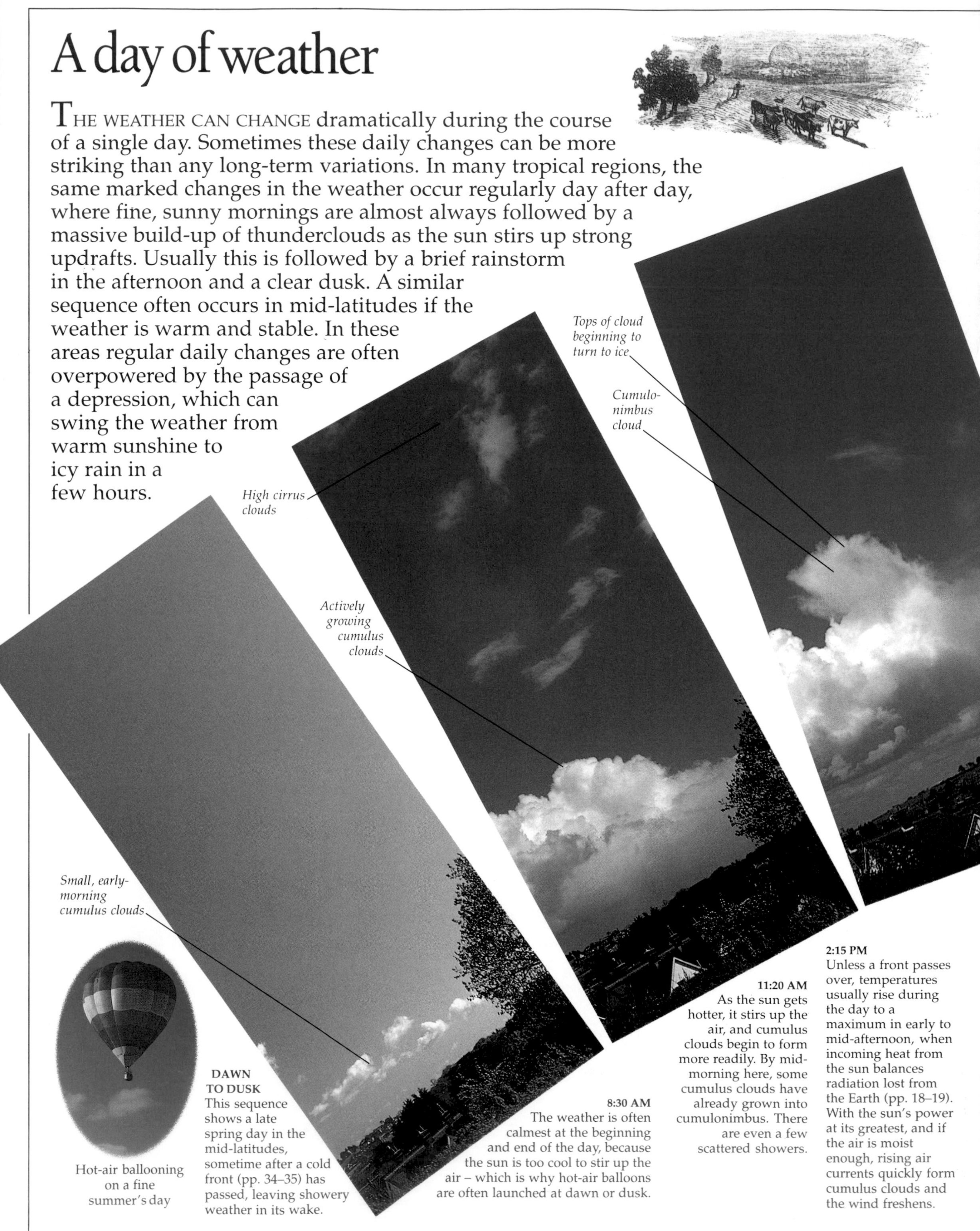

Hot-air ballooning on a fine summer's day

DAWN TO DUSK
This sequence shows a late spring day in the mid-latitudes, sometime after a cold front (pp. 34–35) has passed, leaving showery weather in its wake.

8:30 AM
The weather is often calmest at the beginning and end of the day, because the sun is too cool to stir up the air – which is why hot-air balloons are often launched at dawn or dusk.

11:20 AM
As the sun gets hotter, it stirs up the air, and cumulus clouds begin to form more readily. By mid-morning here, some cumulus clouds have already grown into cumulonimbus. There are even a few scattered showers.

2:15 PM
Unless a front passes over, temperatures usually rise during the day to a maximum in early to mid-afternoon, when incoming heat from the sun balances radiation lost from the Earth (pp. 18–19). With the sun's power at its greatest, and if the air is moist enough, rising air currents quickly form cumulus clouds and the wind freshens.

Icy head of cloud spread out by high level winds

Sky thick with cloud

Rain heavy in places

Sky starting to lighten behind cloud

Rain

3:00 PM
By mid-afternoon, clouds can build up to such an extent that thunderstorms occur. Here, clusters of clouds have joined together to make even larger storms, with thunder and lightning, very heavy rain, and hail nearby, even if not overhead.

3:45 PM
The sky is still darkened by a gigantic, gray cumulonimbus cloud, its top hidden by the widespread lower clouds around the edge of the storm, which is now upon us. Gusts of wind give warning of the downdrafts and torrential rain to come.

5:15 PM
The heavy clouds are beginning to lift and move away, although rain is still falling. Sunlight strikes through beneath the edge of the cloud, illuminating the raindrops and creating a rainbow. The worst of the storm is over.

Extra, pinkish-violet bows inside the primary bow

CASTLES IN THE AIR
In the right conditions, a layer of warm air may form over a cold sea. On the Italian island of Sicily, this can produce a mirage about mid-morning called fata morgana. Distorted images of distant objects appear, looking like castles or tall buildings. They are created when the warm air bends light rays from images of objects normally invisible beyond the horizon.

7:00 PM
By sunset, the wind has dropped and the band of thunderstorms and showers has moved away, leaving only a few scattered cumulus. In contrast to the clear sky of the morning, increasing middle-level clouds show that a weak trough of low pressure is approaching from the west.

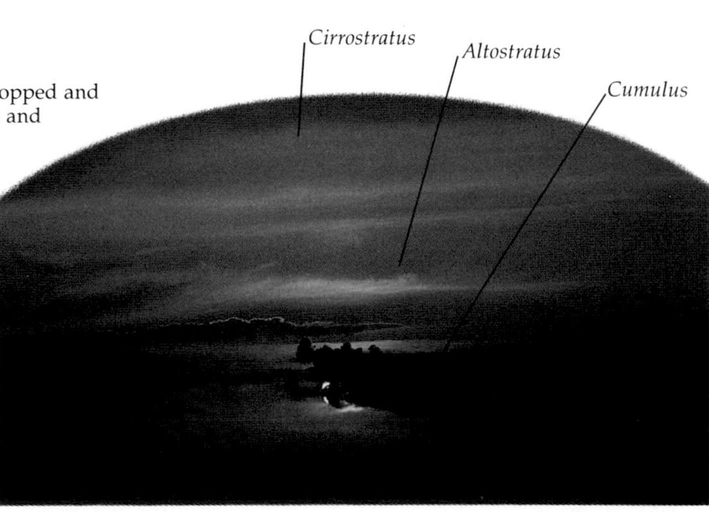

Mountain weather

HIGH UP IN THE ATMOSPHERE, pressure drops, winds are ferocious, and the air is bitterly cold. On high mountaintops, the air pressure can be as low as 300 mb, winds howl through the crags at up to 190 mph (320 kph), and the temperature often drops to -94°F (-70°C). Even on lower mountains, winds tend to be much stronger than down on the plains. Above a certain height – known as the snowline – many mountains are permanently coated in snow and ice. Because mountains jut so far into the atmosphere, they interfere with wind and cloud patterns, forcing air to move up or down as it passes over their peaks. Air rising up the windward side of a mountain – the side facing the wind – means that lower summits are often shrouded in mist and rain.

CLOUDS AND SNOW
In many mountain ranges, the highest peaks may project above the tops of the clouds, basking in bright sunshine while clouds fill the valley below. Only a few icy wisps of clouds may climb to the summits, and the air is dry and clear. Although in sun, the peaks are usually icy cold, and any heat from the sun is reflected straight back into the atmosphere by the snow. Near the equator, only the very highest peaks – above 16,400 ft (5,000 m) or so – are always covered in snow (as it is too cold here for rain). Toward the poles, however, the snow line gets lower.

Barometer used for measuring air pressure

HIGH READINGS
Many weather stations are sited on mountaintops to record conditions high up in the atmosphere, but they are bleak places. On the summit of Mount Washington in New Hampshire, winds are frequently over 95 mph (160 kph), temperatures are often below -22°F (-30°C), and dense fog is common.

PRESSURE AT THE BOTTOM
In 1648, French scientist Blaise Pascal proved Torricelli's view (pp. 10–11) that the atmosphere had its own weight, or pressure. If Torricelli was right, Pascal thought, the air pressure would be lower at the top of a mountain (the Puy-de-Dôme) because there was less air weighing down on it. Pascal, who was in poor health, stayed at the bottom of the mountain with one barometer as his brother-in-law climbed up with another to prove the case.

WET PEAKS
Even when it is not cold, the tops of mountains tend to be wet and misty – especially if they poke up into a moist air stream. Pacific island mountains, like these in Tahiti, are among the dampest places in the world. Hawaii's Mount Wai-'ale-'ale is wreathed in moist clouds for 354 days a year, and is soaked annually by more than 457 in (11,600 mm) of rain.

ALPINE FLOWER
Tiny flowers, called alpines, have adapted well to the sunny, cold weather of mountains such as the Alps in Europe, where they grow plentifully in spring.

HIGH SIERRA
High up in the mountains, a strong wind often increases the effect of the chill in the air, even on the sunniest days. Mountaintops are nearly always windier than low, open country. This is partly because wind strength everywhere increases with height. Winds can be much stronger at 3300 ft (1000 m), than at sea level. Also, winds rush over, rather than around, the tops of mountains, and gain speed as they do so.

AIR LIFT
When a moist air stream meets a mountain range, it is forced upward. As it rises, it cools and may condense into clouds around the summits. Higher-level clouds can then act as "feeder" clouds, letting a little rain fall onto the summit clouds below. Soon the summit clouds are raining heavily. Fronts, too, may be disrupted by mountains. Warm fronts (pp. 32–33) may be broken up when they reach a mountain ridge. Cold fronts (pp. 34–35) may deposit so much rain that they die out quickly on the far side. All this brings rain to the windward side of mountains, and leaves the leeward side (the side not facing the wind) much drier.

Weather on the plains

THE GREAT PLAINS of North America, the steppes of Russia, the pampas of South America, the grasslands of Australia – these and other vast, flat plains of the world experience weather that is very different from that in the mountains (pp. 52–53). Far from the sea, or cut off from it by high mountains, plains tend to have hot summers and cold winters, and receive little rain. Fronts (pp. 32–35) are broken up by mountain ranges or lose their energy long before they reach the heart of the plains. What rain there is falls mostly in the summer, when strong sun stirs up heavy showers and thunderstorms. In winter, rainfall is rare, although autumn snowstorms may deposit a covering that lasts until spring. In the shadow of mountain ranges, many plains are so dry that only scrub, or grass, can grow.

WINTER HUNTERS
Millions of buffalo once roamed the vast grasslands of North America and provided rich hunting for the many Plains Indian tribes, who were well adapted to the cold winters. They would wear snowshoes when hunting so they would not sink into the snow.

HOT BLAST
Plains in the lee of mountains are often subject to hot, dry winds, warmed as they descend from mountains. The chinook of the North American Rockies, and the parching Arabian simoom, shown in this engraving, are typical.

WAVE–CLOUDS
High mountain ranges often disturb winds blowing across them, and set up a pattern of waves that do not move, but hang in the same place in the upper atmosphere. Bands of stationary clouds may form in the crest of each wave.

Skies are often clear, giving hot summers and cold winters

EXTREME WEATHER
Far from any source of moisture, the skies over the plains are often brilliantly clear and blue. This causes natural extremes in temperature between summer and winter, day and night. Winters on the plains are bitter, with temperatures well below freezing and severe frosts for many weeks. In summer, temperatures drop once the sun goes down.

PARCHED LANDS
Most of the world's great deserts are plains, such as North America's Nevada. Air subsiding over the desert warms as it descends, creating parched conditions, and then moves outward, preventing moist air from entering. Mountain ranges produce dry "rain shadows" on their lee (downwind) side.

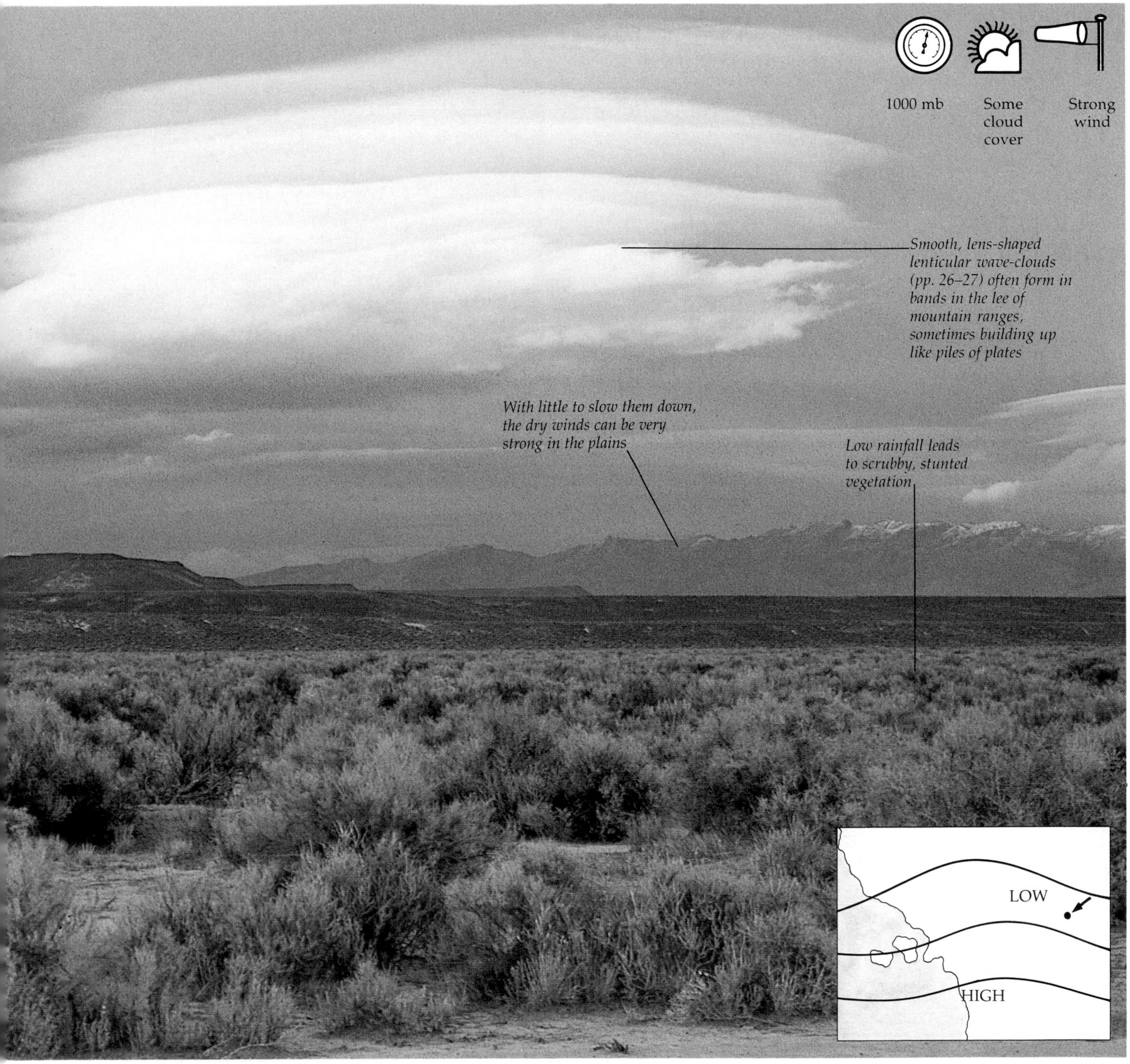

1000 mb

Some cloud cover

Strong wind

Smooth, lens-shaped lenticular wave-clouds (pp. 26–27) often form in bands in the lee of mountain ranges, sometimes building up like piles of plates

With little to slow them down, the dry winds can be very strong in the plains

Low rainfall leads to scrubby, stunted vegetation

LOW

HIGH

DUST TO DUST

Far from the sea, the plains are sensitive to climate changes. Strengthening westerly winds in the early 20th century increased the Rocky Mountains' rainshadow effect on the prairies. Reduced rainfall in the 1930s brought disaster to vast areas, and a "dust bowl" was created by the drought.

SIZZLING SUMMERS

Summer on the plains can be extremely hot. In Death Valley, California (above), temperatures reached 134°F (56.7°C) in 1913. In Queensland, Australia, temperatures soared nearly as high at 127.6°F (53.1°C) in 1889. The highest temperature ever recorded is 136.4°F (58°C) in Libya in 1922.

Weather by the sea

THE PRESENCE OF SO MUCH WATER GIVES weather by the sea its own particular characteristics. Winds blowing in off the sea are naturally moister than those blowing off the land. So coastal areas tend to be noticeably wetter than inland areas – especially if they face into the wind (pp. 42–43). They can be cloudier, too. Cumulus clouds (pp. 24–25), for instance, usually form inland only during the day, but on coasts facing the wind, they drift overhead at night as well, when cold winds blow in over the warm sea. Sometimes these clouds bring localized showers to coastal areas. Fogs too can form at sea in the same way, and creep a little way inland. At daybreak the sea is often shrouded in a thick mist that disperses only as the wind changes or as the sun's heat begins to dry it up. The overall effect of all this water is to make weather in coastal areas generally less extreme than farther inland. Because the sea retains heat well, nights tend to be warmer on the coast, with winters milder, and summers slightly cooler. Frosts are rare on sea coasts in the mid-latitudes.

OUT FOR A BLOW
Seaside resorts are often very windy, as this postcard from the early 20th century acknowledges. The open sea provides no obstacle to winds blowing off the sea, and temperature differences between land and sea can generate stiff breezes as well.

Frequent, salt-laden winds blowing from the sea dry the exposed sides of trees and shrubs, killing leaves and buds, so the plants look as though they are leaning into the wind

CLEAR COAST
This picture shows the coast of Oregon, but it is typical of west coasts everywhere in the mid-latitudes. Deep depressions are common at this latitude, and here a cold front (pp. 34–35) has just passed over, moving inland. An overhang of cloud lingers in the upper air from the front itself, and cumulus clouds are still growing in its wake. More showers are clearly on the way. As the front moves inland, it may well produce progressively less rain, because there is less moisture available to feed its progress.

COASTAL FOG
Sea fog is an advection fog (pp. 48–49), which tends to persist until the direction of the wind changes, because the sea is slow to heat up. Off the coast of Newfoundland in Canada (left), where warm westerly winds blow over a sea cooled by currents flowing down from the Arctic, thick fogs can linger for days on end.

Nighttime land breeze

Daytime sea breeze

WIND AND WAVES
The winds that help windsurfers skim across the surface of the sea may often be locally generated sea breezes. But the waves they ride may be created by winds thousands of miles away. Waves are whipped up by the wind when air turbulence over the water creates little pockets of low and high pressure that suck and push on the water. Just how big the waves are depends on the strength of the wind, how long it blows, and the "fetch" – that is, how far it blows over the water.

Land and sea breezes

A marked characteristic of coastal areas is the frequent occurrence of local wind circulations called land and sea breezes. These are sporadic in mid-latitudes, but in the tropics they blow virtually every day. Both occur because land and water absorb and lose heat from the sun at different rates. During the day, the land heats far more quickly than the sea, and air begins to rise. As warm air rises above the land, cool air from the sea is drawn in underneath, creating a stiff sea breeze, blowing inland. At night, the situation is reversed. The land cools more quickly, and air begins to sink. The cool air pushes out under the warm air over the sea. This is called a land breeze.

Colors in the sky

PURE SUNLIGHT IS WHITE, but it is made up of the seven colors of the rainbow mixed together. As sunlight passes through the atmosphere, gases, dust, ice crystals, and water droplets in the air split it into its rich variety of colors. Clear skies look blue because gases in the air bounce mostly blue light toward our eyes. Sunset skies may be fiery red because the rays of the setting sun travel so far through the dense, lower atmosphere that nearly all colors but red are absorbed. But the endless stirring of the atmosphere by sun and wind constantly brings new colors to the sky. Sometimes, sunlight strikes ice and water in the air to create spectacular effects such as rainbows and triple suns. Rainbows form in showery weather, when there is a break in the clouds after rain, and always appear on the opposite side of the sky to the sun. Occasionally, electrical discharges can bring dramatic color to the sky – particularly at night.

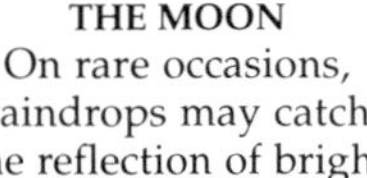

THE COLORS OF THE MOON
On rare occasions, raindrops may catch the reflection of bright moonlight to form a moonbow. The colors of the moonbow are faint, but they are the same as those seen in a rainbow during the daytime.

POLAR LIGHTS
Occasionally, highly charged particles from the sun strike gases in the atmosphere high above the poles to create a spectacular display of colored lights in the night sky. In the northern hemisphere, this is known as the *aurora borealis*; in the southern hemisphere, it is known as the *aurora australis*.

Low, stratus-type clouds in shadow

WRAPPED IN A RAINBOW
Rainbows seem to appear and disappear so miraculously that many cultures believe they have magical properties. To the Navajo Indians of the Southwest the rainbow is a spirit. The spirit is depicted on this blanket around two other supernatural beings, with a sacred maize, or corn, plant in the center.

SAINTLY LIGHT
In thundery weather, sailors occasionally see a strange, glowing ball of light on the masthead. Called St. Elmo's Fire, this is actually an electrical discharge like lightning.

THREE SUNS AT ONCE
A colorful halo, or ring, around the sun is often seen in cirrostratus and, occasionally, high altostratus clouds. This phenomenon is caused by ice crystals in the cloud refracting, or bending, sunlight. Bright "mock suns," or sundogs, may also appear, with long, white tails pointing away from the left or right of the real sun.

MISTY GIANTS
The "Brocken Specter" appears when sunlight projects the enlarged shadows of mountaineers onto low-lying mist or clouds nearby.

WATER COLORS
Rainbows are sunlight that is bent and reflected by raindrops. As the light enters a raindrop, it is bent slightly. It is reflected from the back of the drop and bent again as it leaves the front. It is the bending that separates the white light into its separate colors. Each drop splits light into all of the colors, but they leave the drop at different angles, so you see only one color from a particular drop. The colors are always in the same order: red (on the outside of a primary bow), orange, yellow, green, blue, indigo, and violet.

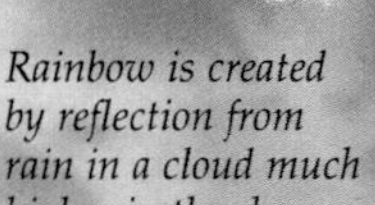

Rainbow is created by reflection from rain in a cloud much higher in the sky

Receding cumulonimbus cloud

Red on the top or outside of a "primary" rainbow

Yellow in the rainbow's center

Violet on the bottom or inside of the rainbow

From aeroplanes, a rainbow can sometimes be seen as a full circle

Our changing weather

THE WORLD'S WEATHER has not always been the same. Since the Earth cooled and acquired its atmosphere some four billion years ago, its climate has gone through many changes, some lasting just a few years, others lasting thousands of years. By far the most dramatic changes have occurred between cold periods (the Ice Ages, or glacials), and warm periods (interglacials). In the last Ice Age, the weather was so cold that the polar ice sheets grew to cover a third of the Earth in ice over 800 ft (240 m) thick. We now live in an interglacial following the end of the last Ice Age, some 10,000 years ago. Since then, there have been many minor changes in the weather. Now, many people believe humans are changing the atmosphere so much that the world is steadily warming up (global warming), endangering our very existence.

FOSSIL AIR
As tree sap solidified into amber long ago, creatures like this spider were trapped along with air bubbles. The air in amber could show what the Earth's atmosphere was once like, but it usually proves to be contaminated.

METEORIC FALL
Dinosaurs dominated the Earth for 250 million years, but they may have been killed off by a catastrophic change in climate. About 65 million years ago, a huge meteor may have struck the Earth, sending up so much dust that the sun's rays were blocked out, making the Earth very cold.

Close rings mean a cold year, far apart, warm

PRESERVED IN ICE
Ice drilled from glaciers reveals what the climate was like when the ice formed. Tiny bubbles of air, frozen within the ice during the Ice Age, show that the atmosphere contained less carbon dioxide, indicating that global warming was less.

PAST WARMTH
The world's coal and oil deposits are the compressed remains of vast forests that grew in the Carboniferous, or coal-bearing, era. The climate of the Carboniferous era was much warmer than it is now.

WOOLLY TIMES
At the end of the last Ice Age, huge elephant-like creatures, called mammoths, roamed near ice sheets far from the poles. They had huge, curling tusks and long, woolly coats to protect them from the cold. A few have been found preserved, frozen almost intact, in Siberia.

GROWING EVIDENCE
Each ring in a cut tree trunk shows one year's growth. If the ring is wide, the tree grew well, and the weather was warm; if narrow, then it was cold.

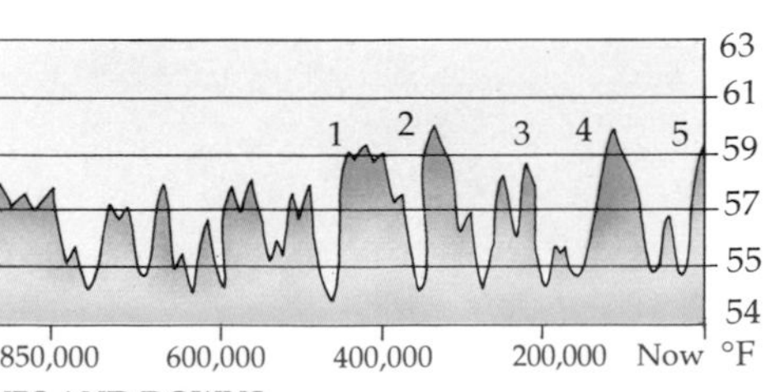

UPS AND DOWNS
Peaks in temperature over the past 850,000 years show five major warm interglacial periods (1–5 on diagram), interspersed by five Ice Ages, when temperatures on Earth were 5°F (3°C) cooler than they are now – cold enough for vast ice sheets to extend halfway through North America, as far as the Alps in Europe, and over New Zealand.

VIKING VOYAGE
Around 1000–1200 A.D., the world's weather became so warm that much of the Arctic ice cap melted. At that time, Viking voyagers were sailing across the Atlantic, settling in Iceland and Greenland, and even reaching America. But the return of cold weather in the "little Ice Age," from 1450 to 1850, brought back the ice sheets, and destroyed the Viking communities in these areas.

WEATHER JOURNAL
Old diaries and weather records, kept by amateur meteorologists, are rich sources of past climates. Such diaries were particularly popular in 18th-century France and England. Among the best were those kept by Thomas Barker in England between 1736 and 1798. His records give an almost complete picture of over 60 years of weather.

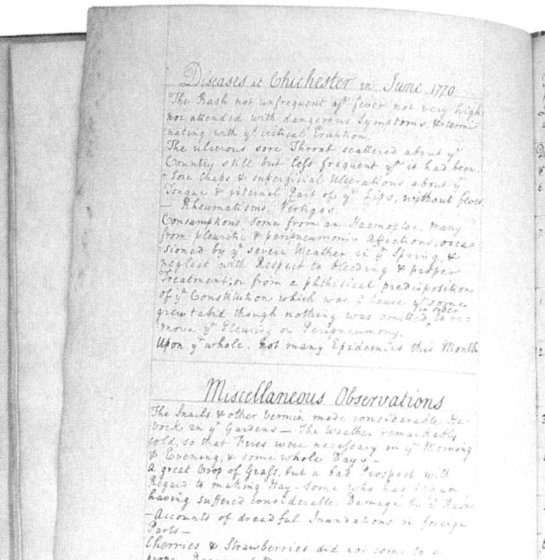
Diseases at Chichester in June 1770

Miscellaneous Observations

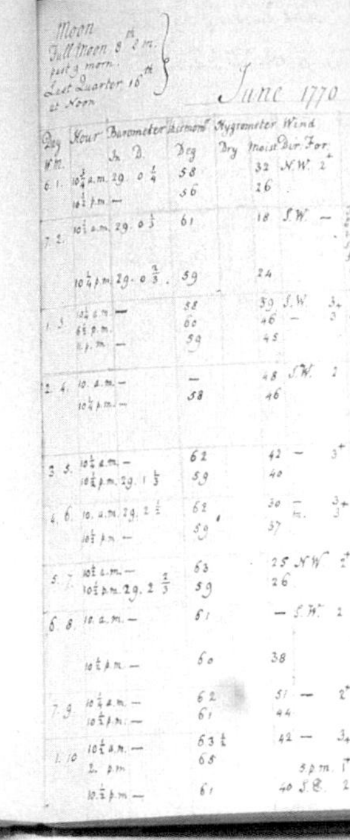
June 1770

HOLE IN THE SKY
Ozone is a bluish gas that occurs naturally in very small quantities high in the atmosphere. It plays a vital role in protecting us from the sun's harmful ultraviolet radiation, which can cause skin cancer and stop plants from growing. Recently, a hole has appeared every spring in the ozone layer over the Antarctic – shown in this satellite photograph – and levels of ozone in the atmosphere are declining. The chemicals causing the damage are being phased out and the ozone should recover.

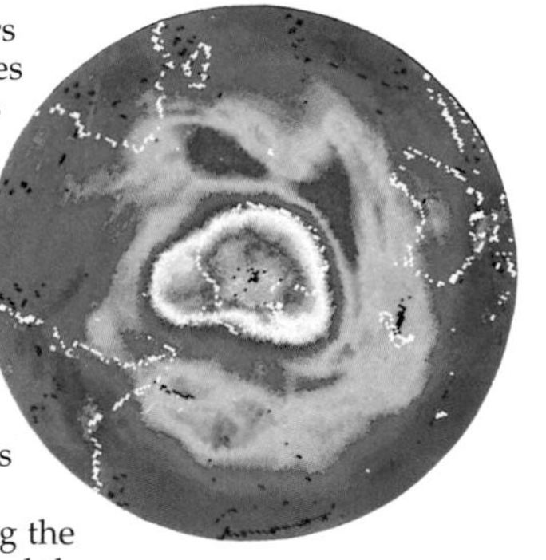

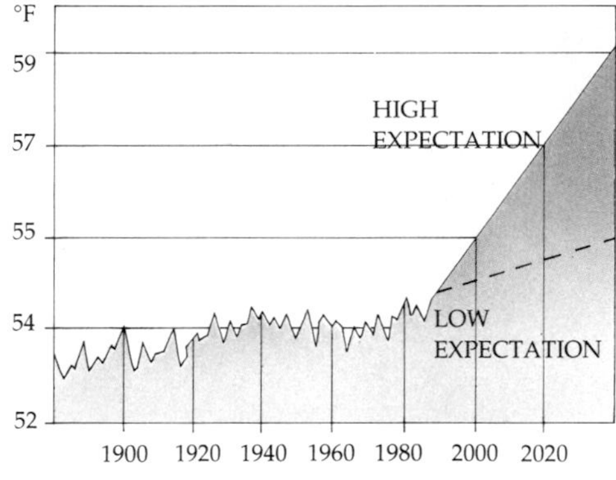

GLOBAL WARMING
Most meteorologists predict that the world will warm between 2.5 and 10.4°F (1.4–5.8°C) by the year 2030, unless we do something drastic to cut down the increase in greenhouse gases.

SATANIC MILLS
Man's effect on the atmosphere really started with the burning of coal in cities in the 16th century. It became worse with the increase in heavy industry in the early 19th century. Smoke from thousands of factory chimneys and soot from millions of coal fires in homes in vast, new cities created a real problem – smog (pp. 48–49).

Climate in crisis

In recent years, people have become increasingly worried about the effects of human activities on the world's weather. Most meteorologists are now convinced that the world is getting warmer, due to increased "greenhouse" gases in the atmosphere – though just how much warmer they cannot agree. Greenhouse gases are beneficial in the right quantities. Like the panes of glass in a greenhouse, they trap heat and keep the Earth snug and warm, but now they are keeping the Earth too warm. Carbon dioxide is the main greenhouse gas, and most of the increase comes from burning coal, oil, and wood, but methane from rice fields and garbage dumps and CFCs from aerosol sprays and refrigerators also contribute to the greenhouse effect. If the Earth becomes just a few degrees warmer, some places may also become drier, making farming more difficult, and wildlife may be harmed.

THE DEATH OF THE FOREST
Every year, tropical forests equivalent to the size of Iceland are cut and burned to make temporary cattle pasture – mostly in Brazil's Amazon basin. Meteorologists are uncertain exactly how this will affect the climate. Rainfall may drop as fewer trees put less moisture into the air. The loss of trees may also increase the greenhouse effect. Forests are made largely from carbon. If they are cleared and burned without being replaced, that carbon is released into the air as carbon dioxide – a "greenhouse gas."

THE CULPRIT
Car and truck exhausts emit all kinds of pollutants, such as nitrous oxide, and vast quantities of the greenhouse gas carbon dioxide.

Home weather station

PROFESSIONAL METEOROLOGISTS have a great deal of sophisticated equipment and thousands of weather stations to help them track the weather (pp. 12–13). But you can keep your own local weather watch with simple instruments – some of which can be made easily at home – and your own eyes. The longer the period over which observations are made, the more interesting and more valuable they become. But you must take measurements at exactly the same time at least once every day, without fail. This way your records can be more easily compared with those made by the professionals. The most important readings are rainfall, temperature range, wind speed and direction, and air pressure. If you can, record the humidity and soil temperature as well, and make a visual estimate of how much of the sky is covered by cloud.

HIGH WINDS
Professional meteorologists have always tried to mount instruments for measuring wind speeds on special masts or high buildings. Here the wind is least affected by obstructions on the ground.

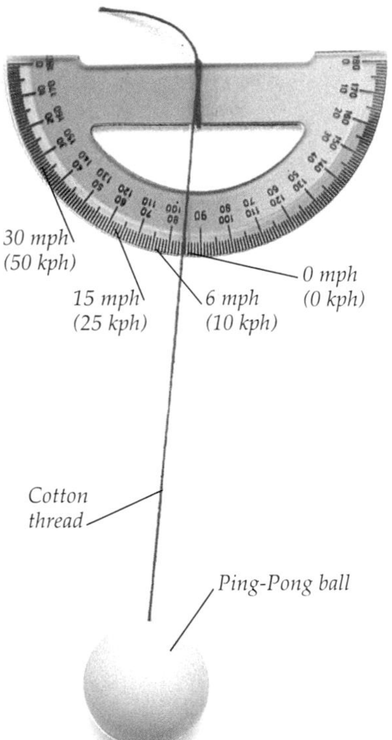

Protractor

30 mph (50 kph)

15 mph (25 kph)

6 mph (10 kph)

0 mph (0 kph)

Cotton thread

Ping-Pong ball

Home-made wind gauge, or anemometer

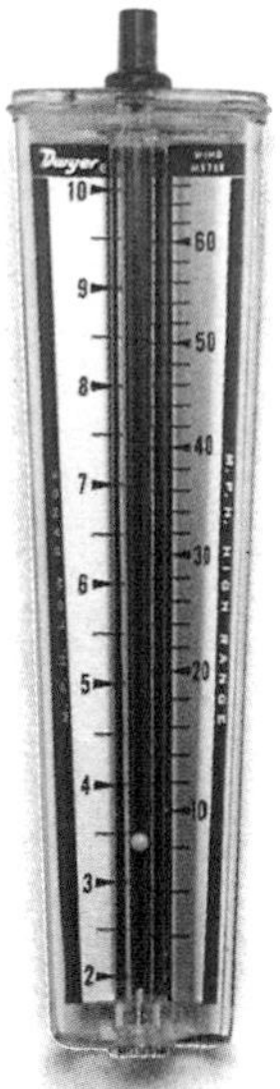

Ventimeter

WIND SPEED
You can roughly measure the wind speed using a Ping-Pong ball glued to the end of a thread that has been tied to the center of a protractor (left). By holding the protractor parallel to the wind, you can read the angle the ball is blown to by the wind and so work out the wind speed. A hand-held, plastic ventimeter (right) is much more accurate, but more expensive.

Air pressure in millibars

Air pressure in inches of mercury

Moving pointer indicating pressure

Pointer to indicate lowest pressure reached

An aneroid barometer has a face like a clock

AIR PRESSURE
A barometer (pp. 10–11) is perhaps the most useful instrument of all, if you want to make forecasts as well as keep records. It clearly shows a drop in pressure bringing storms, and a rise in pressure promising good weather. When a storm approaches, take a reading every 30 minutes to see how fast and how far the pressure falls. Unfortunately, even simple aneroid barometers like this are expensive.

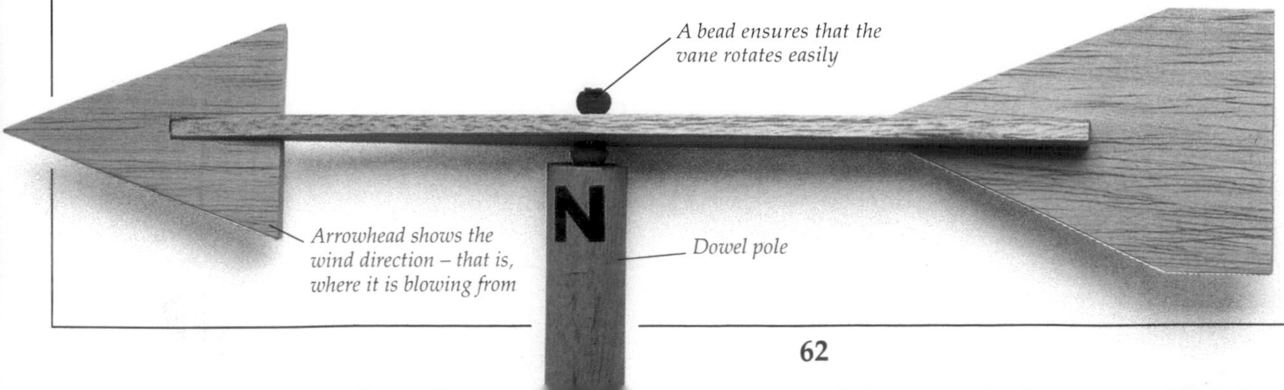

A bead ensures that the vane rotates easily

Arrowhead shows the wind direction – that is, where it is blowing from

Dowel pole

WIND DIRECTION
A weathervane can be made with balsa wood and mounted on a dowel. Make the vane's head smaller than its tail (the pointer indicates where the wind is coming from). Paint it to protect from rain, and use a compass to work out exactly where north and south are.

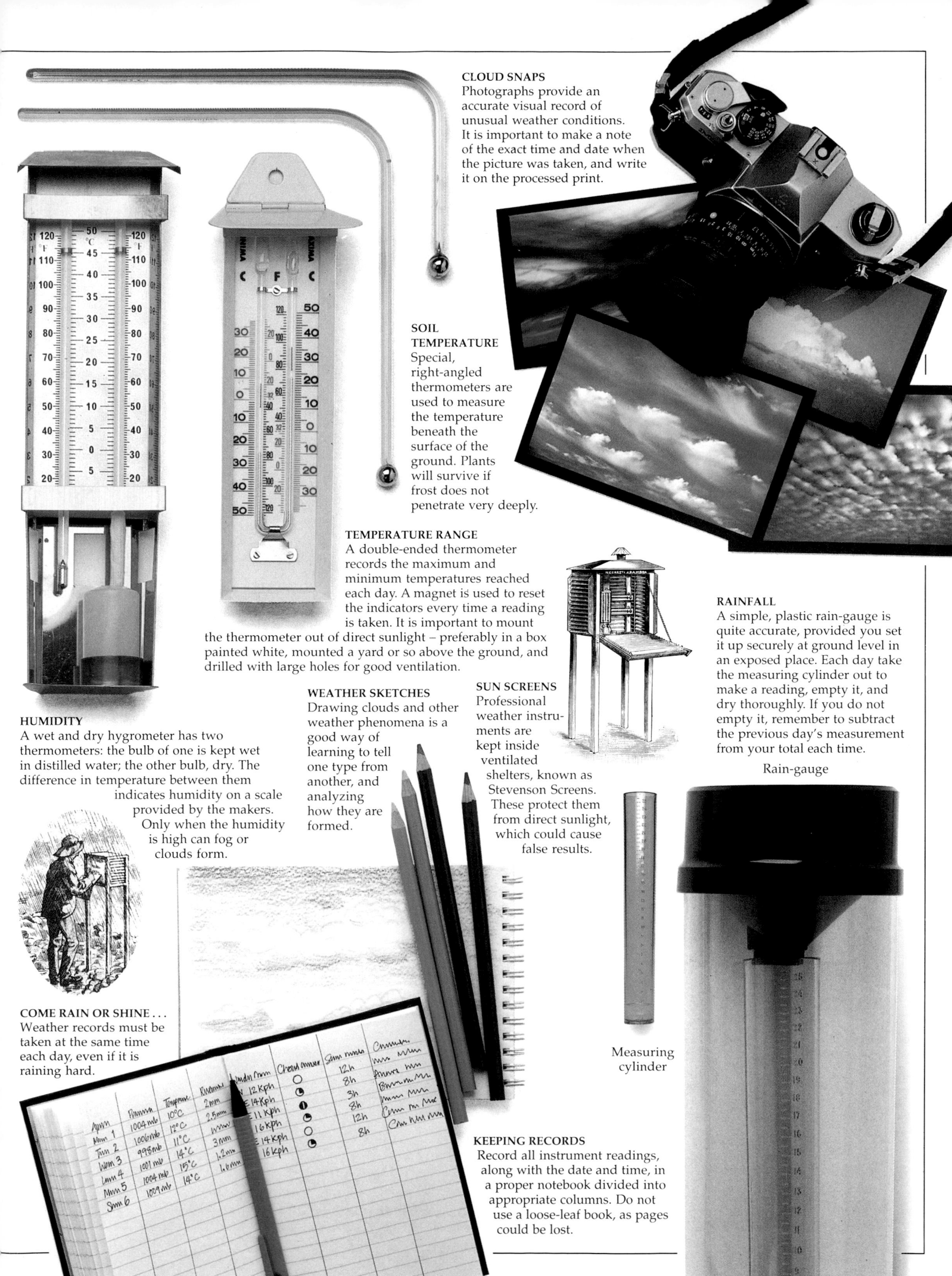

CLOUD SNAPS
Photographs provide an accurate visual record of unusual weather conditions. It is important to make a note of the exact time and date when the picture was taken, and write it on the processed print.

SOIL TEMPERATURE
Special, right-angled thermometers are used to measure the temperature beneath the surface of the ground. Plants will survive if frost does not penetrate very deeply.

TEMPERATURE RANGE
A double-ended thermometer records the maximum and minimum temperatures reached each day. A magnet is used to reset the indicators every time a reading is taken. It is important to mount the thermometer out of direct sunlight – preferably in a box painted white, mounted a yard or so above the ground, and drilled with large holes for good ventilation.

RAINFALL
A simple, plastic rain-gauge is quite accurate, provided you set it up securely at ground level in an exposed place. Each day take the measuring cylinder out to make a reading, empty it, and dry thoroughly. If you do not empty it, remember to subtract the previous day's measurement from your total each time.

Rain-gauge

HUMIDITY
A wet and dry hygrometer has two thermometers: the bulb of one is kept wet in distilled water; the other bulb, dry. The difference in temperature between them indicates humidity on a scale provided by the makers. Only when the humidity is high can fog or clouds form.

WEATHER SKETCHES
Drawing clouds and other weather phenomena is a good way of learning to tell one type from another, and analyzing how they are formed.

SUN SCREENS
Professional weather instruments are kept inside ventilated shelters, known as Stevenson Screens. These protect them from direct sunlight, which could cause false results.

Measuring cylinder

COME RAIN OR SHINE . . .
Weather records must be taken at the same time each day, even if it is raining hard.

KEEPING RECORDS
Record all instrument readings, along with the date and time, in a proper notebook divided into appropriate columns. Do not use a loose-leaf book, as pages could be lost.

Did you know?

AMAZING FACTS

About 12% of the Earth's surface is permanently covered in snow and ice, a total area of about 8 million sq. miles (21 million sq. km). Some 80% of the world's fresh water takes the form of snow or ice, mainly at the North and South Poles.

Frozen waterfall in the Zanskar Range Himalaya Mountains, India

In very cold winters, waterfalls freeze over. Ice grows out from the side of a waterfall as splashed drops of water freeze, one on top of the other. Even Niagara Falls, on the border between the United States and Canada, freezes over.

The atmosphere contains 1.5 billion cubic miles (2.4 billion cubic km) of air and about 34 trillion gallons (15,470 trillion liters) of water. Because of gravity, 80% of the air and nearly all the moisture are in the troposphere, the part of the atmosphere closest to Earth.

Sunbathing can be dangerous on sunny days when there are clouds in the sky. The clouds reflect so much ultraviolet light from the sun that they increase the amount of harmful ultraviolet rays that reach the ground, increasing the risk of skin cancer.

Very hot weather can kill. If it is too hot or humid for people's sweat to evaporate and cool them down, they may get heatstroke. This can lead to collapse, coma, and even death.

The biggest desert in the world is Antarctica. It only has about 5 in (127 mm) of precipitation (snow or rain) a year, just a little more than the Sahara Desert.

It can snow in the desert! Snow sometimes falls during the winter in cold deserts, such as the Great Basin Desert in the United States and the Gobi Desert in Asia.

In 1939, hundreds of frogs, many of them still alive, fell from the sky during a storm in England. They had probably been sucked up from ponds and rivers by small tornadoes, then fell to the ground again with the rain.

Raining frog

A staggering 110 million gallons (500 million liters) of rain can fall from a single thunderstorm.

The average cloud lasts only about ten minutes.

Lenticular cloud

Many reported sightings of UFOs have turned out to be lenticular (lens-shaped) clouds. Waves of wind blowing around mountaintops form smooth, rounded clouds like flying saucers, which hover motionless for hours at a time.

Hailstones sometimes grow to be gigantic. The largest authenticated hailstone in the world fell on Coffeyville, Kansas, in 1970, and weighed 1 lb 11 oz (0.77 kg). A hailstone that was even larger in size (but not in weight) fell in Nebraska in 2003.

Trees in forests around the world are being destroyed by acid rain. Acid rain forms when pollutants from factories and cars interact with sunlight and water vapor in the clouds to form sulfuric and nitric acids. These contaminate water supplies and damage forests and crops.

Conifers destroyed by acid rain

QUESTIONS AND ANSWERS

Q Why does the weather keep changing all the time?

A The heat of the sun keeps the lower atmosphere constantly moving. How much the sun heats the air varies across the world, throughout the day and through the year. These variations mean that the weather is constantly changing.

Q What makes the wind blow?

A Winds blow wherever there is a difference between air temperature and pressure. They always blow from an area of high pressure to an area of low pressure.

Solar corona

Q Why are there sometimes colored rings around the sun?

A Fuzzy, colored rings around the sun are called a solar corona. They appear when the sun is covered by a thin layer of clouds. The water droplets in the clouds split the sunlight, creating a rainbow effect.

Q What makes a large, bright disk around the moon ?

A A lunar corona occurs when sunlight reflected from the moon passes through the water droplets in thin clouds.

Pillars of rock called hoodoos

Q How has the weather made desert rocks such strange shapes?

A Over time, desert rocks are worn away by the weather. Temperature changes and water make rocks crack and shatter. Also, windblown sand acts like sandpaper. It wears away softer rock leaving strange shapes, such as pillars and arches.

Q Why are some deserts hot in the day and freezing cold at night?

A Above hot deserts, the skies are clear. The ground becomes baking hot by day because there are no clouds to shield it, but it turns cold at night because there is nothing to trap the heat, which is lost back into the atmosphere.

Q What is a mirage and where do they appear?

A Mirages are tricks of the light created by very hot air. Air close to the ground is much hotter than the air above it, and light bends as it passes from one temperature to the other. This creates a shimmering reflection that looks like water. Deserts are renowned for producing mirages that look like oases.

Desert mirage

Q How big do the biggest clouds grow?

A The biggest clouds are cumulonimbus, the big, dark rain clouds that often produce thunderstorms. They can be up to 6 miles (9.7 km) high and hold half a million tons of water.

Q Where is the best place to see the tops of clouds?

A Airplanes usually fly above the clouds, and the tops of mountains are sometimes above the clouds.

Q How powerful is the average thunderstorm?

A A typical thunderstorm about 0.6 miles (1 km) across has about the same amount of energy as 10 atom bombs.

Q When is the best time to see a rainbow?

A The best rainbows often appear in the morning or late afternoon, when the sun is out and rain is falling in the distance. Stand with your back to the sun and look toward the rain to see the rainbow. The lower the sun is in the sky, the wider the bow will be.

Record Breakers

THE COLDEST PLACE:
The lowest temperture ever recorded was -128.6°F (-89.2°C) at Vostok Station, Antarctica, on July 21, 1983.

THE HOTTEST PLACE:
At Al'Aziziyah, Libya, the temperature reached a record high of 136°F (58°C), on September 13, 1922.

THE DRIEST PLACE:
Arica in Chile's Atacama Desert is the driest recorded place on Earth, with less than 0.03 in (0.75 mm) of rain a year for 59 years.

THE WETTEST PLACE:
Lloro, Colombia, is the rainiest place in the world, receiving an average 525 in (1,330 cm) of rain a year for 29 years.

THE FASTEST WINDS:
The fastest winds on Earth are inside the funnel of a tornado. They spin at speeds of up to 300 miles (480 km) an hour.

Working with weather

IN RECENT YEARS, scientists have become increasingly worried that human activities may be changing the climate. Meteorologists are constantly doing research into the weather, often in dangerous conditions, to make long-range predictions viable. To reduce emissions of pollutant gases, scientists are also harnessing the power of the weather to provide cleaner, alternative sources of energy.

La Rance tidal barrage, France

TIDAL POWER
The energy of the tides can be harnessed by building a barrage across a suitable estuary. As the water flows in and out twice a day, it passes through turbines, which generate clean, renewable electricity. The biggest tidal energy plant in the world crosses the La Rance estuary in Brittany, France. It provides electricity for 25,000 households.

The aircraft are equipped with data-gathering instruments.

The WC-130 normally carries a crew of six people.

US Air Force WC-130 aircraft

HURRICANE HUNTERS
An Air Force squadron known as the Hurricane Hunters flies aircraft through hurricanes to monitor them and predict when and where they will hit land. The specially adapted aircraft fly through a hurricane in an X pattern, passing through the eye every two hours, and transmit information by satellite to the National Hurricane Center. The air crews can detect dangerous changes in a hurricane's intensity and movement that are hard to predict by satellite alone.

TORNADO ALLEY
Tornadoes are more common in the United States than anywhere else. They strike regularly in an area known as Tornado Alley, which is made up of the states between South Dakota and Texas.

Number of tornadoes per 50 miles square (80 km sq)

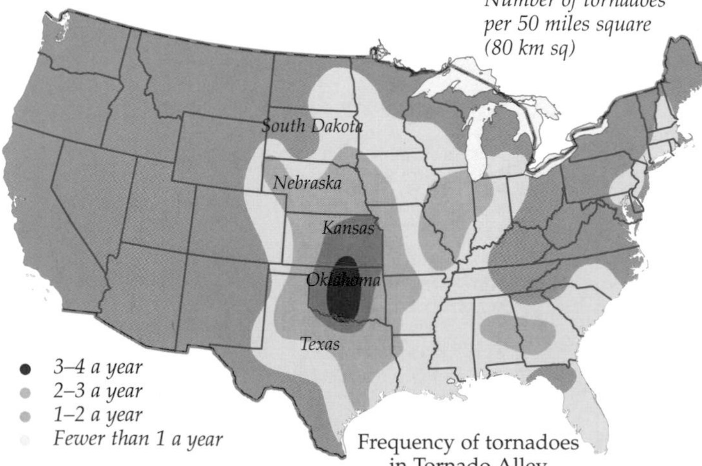

Frequency of tornadoes in Tornado Alley

GENERAL WEATHER WEB SITES

- An excellent starting point for finding out about weather from the National Weather Service: **www.nws.noaa.gov/om/reachout/kidspage.shtml**
- A weather Web site that answers common questions and suggests kid-friendly experiments: **www.ucar.edu/40th/webweather/**
- A weather Web site featuring weather-related activities, stories, and games: **www.ucar.edu/educ_outreach/webweather/**

Prairie tornado photograph taken by a storm chaser

STORM CHASERS
Some scientists risk their lives by studying tornadoes at close range. These storm chasers use Doppler radar dishes that enable them to look right inside storm clouds to see signs of a developing tornado. Their research helps forecasters to give advance warning of danger.

LIFE IN THE FREEZER

Meteorologists and other scientists based at various research stations in Antarctica study changing climate conditions in detail. They also monitor the seasonal hole in the ozone layer that lies above Antarctica to find out how pollution and our efforts to prevent it are affecting the atmosphere.

Scientist launching a weather balloon

Meteorologist servicing an automatic weather station

ANTARCTIC RESEARCH

In Antarctica, meteorologists carry out experiments to improve the quality of weather forecasts and to make long-term predictions about climate change. Other scientists study the ice sheet for valuable information about climate changes in the past and the effects of current global warming. Oceanographers, geologists, and biologists research the changing ocean conditions in the icy seas around Antarctica and their effects on plant and animal life.

SOLAR POWER

The Sun is potentially the most powerful source of renewable energy. Solar power stations aim to capture this energy by using thousands of wide mirrors to collect and concentrate as much sunlight as possible. Luz, in California's Mojave Desert, has the biggest solar power station in the world: 650,000 enormous solar mirrors reflect heat onto tubes filled with oil. The hot oil heats water, which in turn makes steam. This drives turbines that generate electricity.

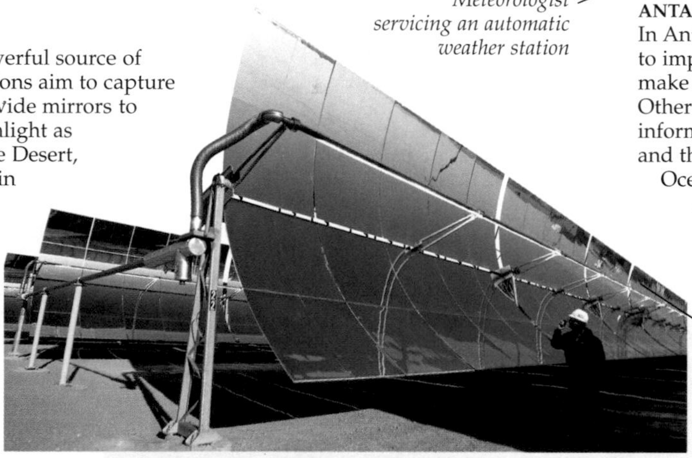

Each of these mirrors is computer controlled to track the Sun across the sky during the day.

Wind farm near Palm Springs, California

CATCHING THE WIND

At wind farms, windmills convert the wind's energy into electricity. The windmills have to be far enough apart not to steal wind from one another. Wind farms only work in exposed places, and it takes about 3,000 windmills to generate as much power as a coal power station.

Find out more

- You can find out about hurricane hunters at: **www.hurricanehunters.com**
- For information on storm chasers, visit: **www.stormchaser.com**
- Get information about blizzards, whiteouts, and other weather phenomena: **www.antarcticconnection.com/antarctic/weather/index.shtml**
- Learn about "El Nino" from the National Oceanic and Atmospheric Administration: **www.pmel.noaa.gov/tao/elnino/1997.html**
- You could also visit a science center to learn more about weather. Once such center is Liberty Science Center in New Jersey: **www.lsc.org**

Extreme weather

WEATHER CAN BE VIOLENT and cause extensive damage. Every year, devastating floods, savage storms, blizzards, and prolonged periods of drought occur in different parts of the world, causing renewed speculation about climate change.

STORMS AND FLOODS

FLOODS

Floods cause more damage than any other natural phenomenon. They turn vast areas of dry land into massive lakes, destroying crops and making thousands of people homeless. In February 2000, freak rain in southern Africa caused the worst floods for 50 years in Mozambique. More than a million people had to leave their homes. Before the waters had receded, a cyclone hit the country, making the situation even worse.

Floods at Fenton, Missouri

Flood victims wait to be airlifted from rooftops near Chokwe, Mozambique

HURRICANES

Katrina, a Category-5 hurricane that formed over the Atlantic in late 2005, caused incredible devastation when it struck the Gulf Coast of the US, especially to New Orleans and other parts of Louisiana. Katrina brought ferocious winds, torrential rain, and gigantic tidal surges. It caused the deaths of around 1,800 people, making it one of the deadliest hurricanes ever in the history of the United States.

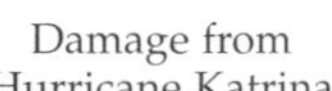

Damage from Hurricane Katrina

THE DUST BOWL

In a dust storm, towering walls of choking dust reach right up to the sky and blot out the sun, creating a ghostly yellow light. In the 1930s, the North American Midwest had no rain for five years, and thousands of acres of fertile prairie grasslands were transformed into a desert known as the Dust Bowl. Hot winds tore across the land, causing suffocating dust storms, and about 5,000 people died as a result of heatstroke and breathing problems.

FIRE, SNOW, AND LANDSLIDES

The eruption of Mount St. Helens, Washington

VOLCANIC WEATHER
Large volcanic eruptions affect the weather worldwide. When Mount St. Helens, Washington, erupted in spring 1980, the entire top of the mountain was blown off. Ash from the volcano was carried by high winds around the planet, leading to hazy skies, amazing sunsets, and a brief drop in temperature. The eruption of Mount Pinatabu, Philippines, in 1999 caused a drop in temperature of 0.9°F (0.5°C) around the world.

WILDFIRE
Raging forest fires are often ignited when lightning strikes vegetation that has been parched by hot, dry weather. Australia has about 15,000 bush fires a year, but on February 16, 1983, now known as Ash Wednesday, a searing heatwave triggered hundreds of fires in different places all at the same time. Driven by strong winds, the fires spread at terrifying speed, engulfing a town, killing 70 people, and damaging thousands of acres of land.

AVALANCHES
When heavy snow builds up on a steep slope, even a small vibration can trigger an avalanche. In winter 1999, the European Alps had mild weather followed by record snowfalls and strong winds. In Austria, a block of snow weighing 187,000 tons (170,000 metric tons) broke away from a mountain and crashed down to the village of Galtür below, killing more than 30 people.

Rescuers using poles to search for victims of the Austrian avalanche

Avalanche on Mount McKinley, Alaska

MUDSLIDES
Every five to seven years, a change in the wind drives an ocean current called El Niño toward the coast of South America, causing violent storms and torrential rain in some areas and drought in others. In December 1999, 10,000 people were killed in Venezuela by floods and huge mudslides. Torrential rain soaked into the hillsides causing the mudslides, which destroyed all buildings, roads and trees in their path.

Mudslides at La Guaira, Venezuela

Glossary

AIR MASS A large body of air covering much of a continent or ocean in which the temperature, surface pressure, and humidity are fairly constant.

AIR PRESSURE The force of air pressing down on the ground or any other horizontal surface. It is sometimes also called atmospheric pressure.

ANEMOMETER An instrument for measuring the speed of the wind.

ANTICYCLONE Also known as a "high," this is a body of air in which the air pressure is higher than it is in the surrounding air.

ATMOSPHERE The layer of gases surrounding the Earth, stretching about 600 miles (1,000 km) into space. All weather takes place in the lowest layer.

AURORA Bands of colored light that appear in the night sky. In the northern hemisphere this phenomenon is called the northern lights or the aurora borealis; in the southern hemisphere, it is called the aurora australis.

BAROGRAPH An instrument that provides a continuous record of air pressure on a strip of paper wound around a revolving drum.

Barograph

BAROMETER An instrument for measuring air pressure. The most accurate type is the mercury barometer, which measures the distance pressure forces mercury up a glass tube containing a vacuum.

BLIZZARD A wind storm in which snow is blown into the air by strong winds at speeds of at least 35 mph (56 kph), reducing visibility to less than ¼ mile (400 m).

CIRRUS Feathery cloud that forms at high altitudes, where the air is very cold.

CLIMATE The normal pattern of weather conditions in a particular place or region, averaged over a long period of time.

CLOUDS Masses of condensed water vapor and ice particles floating in the sky. Ten types of cloud have been categorized, all based on three basic cloud forms: cumulus, stratus, and cirrus.

COLD FRONT The boundary line between warm and cold air masses with the cold air moving toward the area of warm air in front of it.

CONDENSATION The change from a gas, such as water vapor, to a liquid, such as water.

CONVECTION The transfer of heat by the vertical movement of air or water. It makes warm air rise.

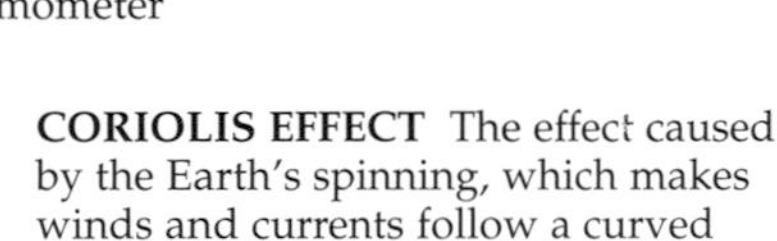

Anemometer

CORIOLIS EFFECT The effect caused by the Earth's spinning, which makes winds and currents follow a curved path across the Earth's surface.

CUMULONIMBUS The type of cloud that produces heavy showers, thunderstorms, and tornadoes. It is bigger and darker than cumulus.

CUMULUS Large, fluffy clouds with flat bases and rounded tops often seen in sunny weather. They often mass together.

CYCLONE Also known as a "low," this is a body of air in which the air pressure is lower than it is in the surrounding air. It is also the name used to describe a hurricane in the Indian Ocean and Western Pacific.

DEPRESSION A weather system where there is a center with low pressure. It is also sometimes known as a cyclone.

DEW Moisture in the air that has condensed on objects at or near the Earth's surface.

DEW POINT The temperature at which water vapor in the air will condense.

DRIZZLE Light rain made of drops that are smaller than 0.02 in (0.5 mm) across.

FOG Water that has condensed from water vapor into tiny droplets near the ground, reducing visibility to around 1,000 yd (1,000 m).

FRONT The boundary between two air masses with different basic characteristics.

Hygrometer

FROST White ice crystals that form on cold surfaces when moisture from the air freezes.

GALE A very strong wind that blows at speeds of 32-63 mph (52-102 kph).

GLOBAL WARMING A long-term increase in the temperature of the atmosphere, possibly caused by the greenhouse effect.

GREENHOUSE EFFECT The warming up of the Earth's surface, caused by radiation from the Sun being trapped by gases in the lower atmosphere, just as heat is trapped in a greenhouse by the glass roof.

GUST A sudden temporary increase in wind speed.

HAIL Rounded drops of ice that fall from clouds.

HEMISPHERE Half of the Earth. There are northern and southern hemispheres.

HOAR FROST Spikes of frost that form when the air is about 32°F (0°C) and water vapor touches the surfaces of trees.

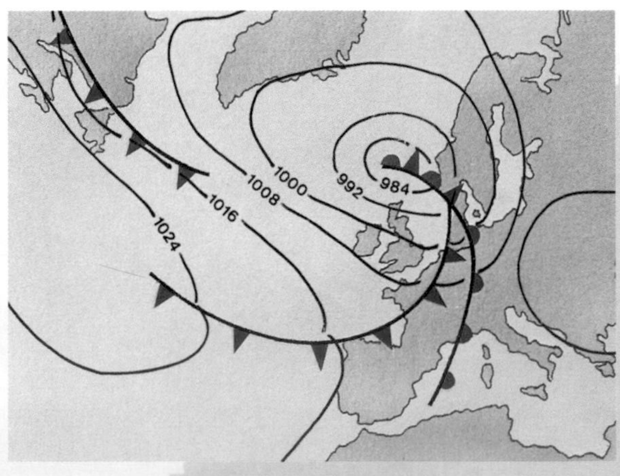

Weather chart showing fronts and isobars

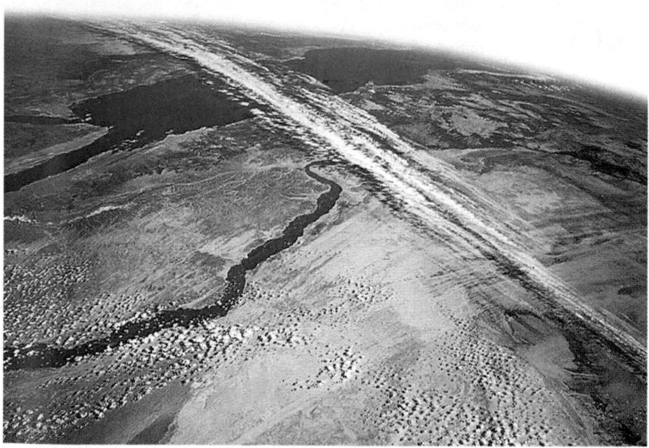

Jet stream clouds

METEOROLOGY The scientific study of weather, both in the atmosphere and at the surface of the Earth.

MILLIBAR The unit that is usually used by meteorologists when measuring and reporting atmospheric pressure.

MONSOON The seasonal shift in wind direction that makes wet seasons alternate with very dry seasons in India and Southeast Asia.

SMOG Originally, fog mixed with smoke, but now more commonly a haze that forms in polluted air in strong sunshine.

SNOW Ice crystals that fall from clouds in cold weather and which may stick together to form snowflakes.

STORM Strong winds, between gale and hurricane force, of 64-75 mph (103-121 kph), which uproot trees and overturn cars.

STRATOSPHERE The layer of the Earth's atmosphere above the troposphere.

STRATUS A vast, dull type of low-level cloud that forms in layers.

SUNSHINE RECORDER An instrument used to record the number of hours of sunshine in a day.

HUMIDITY The amount of water vapor that is in the air.

HURRICANE A tropical cyclone that occurs in the Caribbean and North Atlantic with winds of over 75 mph (121 kph) blowing around a center of air at very low pressure.

HYGROMETER An instrument used for measuring humidity.

ISOBAR A line on a weather map that joins places with the same air pressure.

JET STREAM A band of very strong winds in the upper atmosphere, occasionally blowing at over 200 mph (320 kph).

LIGHTNING A visible discharge of static electricity from a cloud. Sheet lightning is a flash within a cloud. Fork lightning is a flash between a cloud and the ground.

OCCLUDED FRONT A front, or boundary, where cold air undercuts warm air, lifting it clear of the ground.

OZONE LAYER A thin layer of ozone gas in the upper atmosphere that filters out harmful ultraviolet radiation from the Sun before it reaches the Earth.

PRECIPITATION All forms of water that fall to the ground or form on or near it, such as rain, snow, dew, and fog.

PREVAILING WIND The main direction from which the wind blows in a particular place.

RADIATION A process by which energy travels across space as electromagnetic waves, such as light and heat.

RADIOSONDE An instrument package that is sent into the upper atmosphere attached to a weather balloon. It radios weather information back to a receiving station on the ground.

RAIN GAUGE An instrument that is used to collect and measure the amount of rainfall.

RAIN SHADOW An area of decreased rainfall on the lee, or sheltered, side of a hill or mountain.

RIDGE An elongated area of high air pressure.

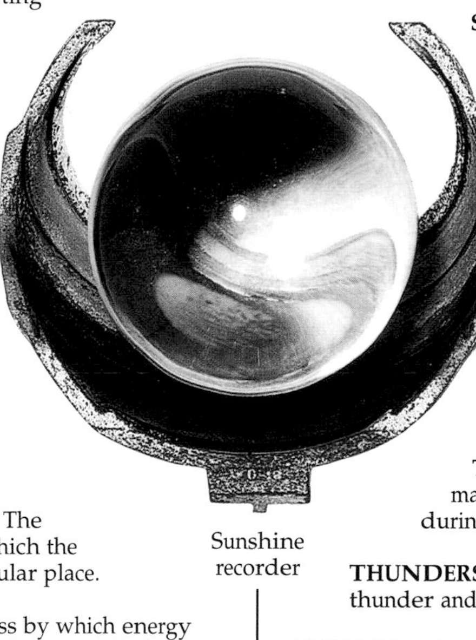

Sunshine recorder

SYNOPTIC CHART A weather chart that provides detailed information about weather conditions at a particular time over a large area.

THERMAL A rising current of warm air.

THERMOSPHERE The top layer of the atmosphere, above about 55 miles (90 km).

THUNDER The sound made by expanding air during a flash of lightning.

THUNDERSTORM A rainstorm with thunder and lightning.

TORNADO A narrow spiral of air rotating at high speed around an area of extremely low air pressure. Wind speeds may be higher than 200 mph (320 kph).

TROPOSPHERE The innermost layer of the Earth's atmosphere, where most of the weather takes place.

TROUGH An elongated area of low pressure.

TYPHOON A tropical cyclone that occurs over the Pacific Ocean.

WARM FRONT A boundary line between two air masses where the air behind the front is warmer than the air ahead of it.

WATERSPOUT A column of rapidly spiraling air that forms over warm and usually shallow water, or when a tornado crosses water.

WIND CHILL The sensation that the air temperature is lower than it really is because of the effect of the wind.

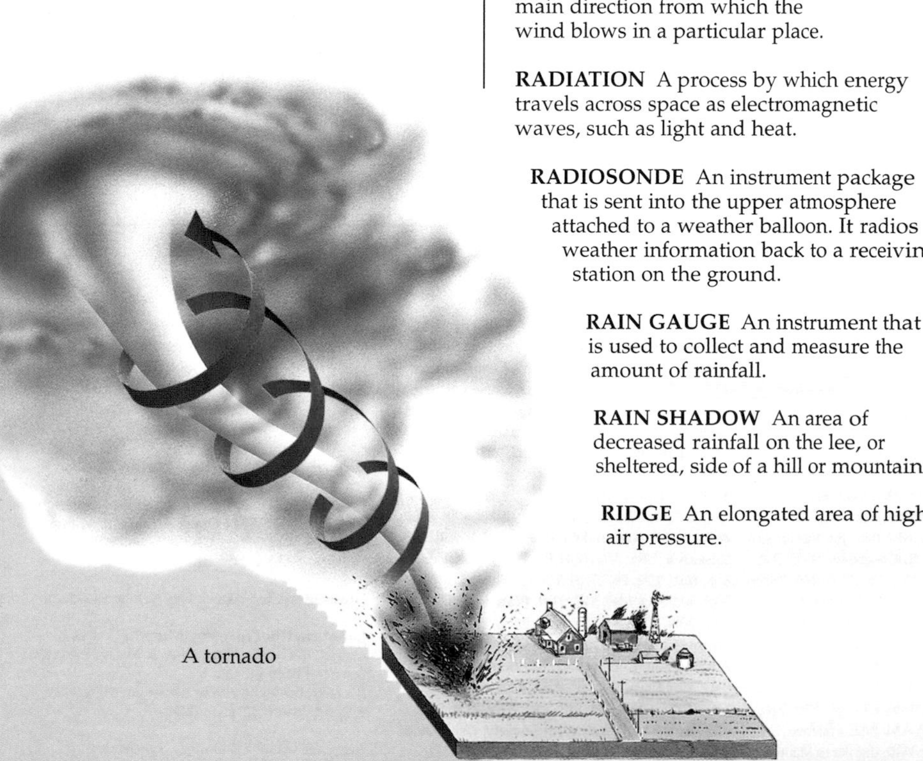

A tornado

AFRICA
AMERICAN REVOLUTION
AMPHIBIAN
ANCIENT CHINA
ANCIENT EGYPT
ANCIENT GREECE
ANCIENT ROME
ARCHEOLOGY
ARCTIC & ANTARCTIC
ARMS & ARMOR
ASTRONOMY
AZTEC, INCA & MAYA
BASEBALL
BASKETBALL
BATTLE
BIBLE LANDS
BIRD
BOAT
BOOK
BUDDHISM
BUILDING
BUTTERFLY & MOTH
CAR
CASTLE
CAT
CHEMISTRY
CHINA
CHRISTIANITY
CIVIL WAR
CLIMATE CHANGE
COSTUME
COWBOY
CRIME & DETECTION
CRYSTAL & GEM
DANCE
DA VINCI & HIS TIMES
DESERT
DINOSAUR
DOG
EAGLE & BIRDS OF PREY
EARLY HUMANS
EARTH
ECOLOGY
ELECTRICITY
ELECTRONICS
ELEPHANT
ENERGY
EPIDEMIC
EVEREST
EVOLUTION
EXPLORER
FARM
FILM
FIRST LADIES
FISH
FLAG
FLYING MACHINE
FOOD
FOOTBALL
FORCE & MOTION
FORENSIC SCIENCE
FOSSIL
FUTURE
GORILLA, MONKEY & APE
GOYA
GREAT MUSICIANS
GREAT SCIENTISTS
HORSE
HUMAN BODY
HURRICANE & TORNADO
IMPRESSIONISM
INDIA
INSECT
INVENTION
ISLAM
JUDAISM
JUNGLE
KNIGHT
LIFE
LIGHT
MAMMAL
MANET
MARS
MATTER
MEDIA & COMMUNICATION
MEDICINE
MEDIEVAL LIFE
MESOPOTAMIA
MONET
MONEY